PARTNERSHIP

PARTNERSHIP

God's **Way** for
Success, Prosperity,
and **Survival**

IZAK J. BESTER

This book was printed in the United States of America.

To order additional copies of this book, contact:
Xlibris Corporation
1-888-795-4274
www.Xlibris.com
Orders@Xlibris.com
57603

Editor-in-Chief: Michele Bester

CONTENTS

PROLOGUE

E pluribus unum: out of many, one. That phrase has long been a part of the great seal of the United States, originally suggested by our Founders in the First Continental Congress. It is a recognition that out of all our different backgrounds, our focus should be on what we have in common: that we are one as Americans. We are to bring our different strengths, pool our efforts, and thereby achieve greater things together than we could ever achieve on our own. Our Founders, having just achieved victory over the most powerful military force on earth at the time, clearly understood the power of unity in overcoming great odds.

Yet today we have reversed the focus of that phrase. No longer are we united Americans, but now we are hyphenated Americans: African Americans, Mexican Americans, Latin Americans. Our focus is more about our differences rather than what we have in common. We live in a world that is getting more and more divisive. Political discourse between liberals and conservatives is nearly nonexistent. Cultural differences have served to separate us further than at any time in our history since the Civil War. Churches can't even seem to get along, not only divided by denominational differences but also by differences within denominations. We see each other in terms of "us" versus "them" rather than just "us." Barriers of disdain and misunderstanding have grown ever stronger between rich and poor, white and black, believer and nonbeliever.

More than ever, we need to come back together; we need to unify and understand the importance of doing so. Therein lies the significance of this book. Izak Bester is not just a personal friend and mentor; he is also a great Bible scholar. When he teaches on a subject that the Lord has laid upon his heart, he does so thoroughly and with deep reflection. This work is no exception. What it means for Christians to partner together, the value of doing so, and the various implications that arise from that bond of unity are all covered in this power-packed book. This book will challenge you, yet it will also equip and empower you to take the steps of faith you need to better accomplish the calling God has on your life.

As this book reminds us, if we are in Christ, we are co-laborers in Christ. We are partners in a great and noble quest to honor our King. That divine mission cannot be accomplished alone or in our own efforts. We were designed to work together, in partnership, reflecting the very nature of our Creator. The late missionary to the Philippines Bishop Charles Henry Brent captured the importance of unity and partnership amongst Christians with the following words that still ring true today:

> *The unity of Christendom is not a luxury, but a necessity. The world will go limping until Christ's prayer that all may be one is answered. We must have unity, not at all costs, but at all risks. A unified Church is the only offering we dare present to the coming Christ, for in it alone will He find room to dwell.*

The sooner we recognize our individual callings in Christ are part of a greater overall plan of our Creator, the sooner we will reflect what our Founders understood so well; *E pluribus unum!*

Douglas S. Anderson, Attorney-at-Law
President and Cofounder of America Reclaimed Ministries
Lt. Col. Air Force (Retired)

INTRODUCTION

This book had its origin in a two-page letter, but as is often the case with God, however, He intended much more. Like most people, I thought I understood partnership, but that was before the Lord took me on a wonderful journey of discovering—yet again and to a depth I never imagined—His blueprint for our survival and continuous prosperity as individuals, as well as Christian communities.

Throughout the writing of this book, I have been led step by step, guided by the Lord and the Holy Spirit in a beautiful, new, refreshing way. He has, once again, showed His heart, His desire, and His intent of partnership with His creation for the purpose of multiplying His Presence and His Kingdom in every aspect of our lives and our society.

The writing of this book comes at no better time. The Bible is clear that in the last days, many will fall away from the faith because false doctrines and false teachers lead them astray. What this denotes is that there are many well-meaning Christians out there who say they love the Lord with all their hearts and who even say they will never deny their Lord, but in the end they will not inherit the Kingdom of God because they are following after charismatic teachers, preachers, pastors, ministries, and prophets instead of staying the course with God. Man is fallible; God is not. In our walk with God, we are to, first and foremost, be in partnership with the Lord Jesus and then anyone else the Holy Spirit directs us to after that.

One of the great things about a civilized society is the sheer abundance of information on any topic you can imagine—right at the press of a button. There are books and writings on every subject. There is a church on every corner. There are conferences and seminars being held all the time. There are more "prophets" and "prophetic ministries" flooding the Christian sector now more than ever. But how many of these things are really, truly of God and are adequately feeding God's people versus giving them "fast food"?

In Matthew, Jesus tells the parable of the seeds sown in different kinds of soil. The Amplified version of Matthew 13:18-21 is so descriptive of many in our churches today:

> *Listen then to the parable of the sower. While any one is hearing the Word of the Kingdom and does not grasp and comprehend it, the evil one comes and snatches away what is sown in his heart. This is what was sown along the roadside. As for what was sown on thin (rocky) soil, this is he who hears the Word and at once welcomes and accepts it with joy; yet it has no real root in himself, but is temporary—inconstant, lasts but a little while and when affliction or trouble or persecution comes on account of the Word, at once he is caused to stumble—he is repelled and begins to distrust and desert Him Whom he ought to trust and obey, and he falls away.*

We have become a "fast food society," even with our faith and religion. There are many parallels between our eating habits in the U.S. and our physical health as a nation, and our "eating habits" and spiritual health as a nation. Most fast foods are high in calorie, high in fat, and/or high in sugar, with the last two being addictive in nature, i.e. the more you eat, the more you crave. Most of this fast food is also nutrient poor, creating a deficit within the body, which ultimately creates a craving for more food. You see, if you don't get the right food and nutrients, you will constantly stay hungry because—even though your mind does not grasp this—your body, your cells are trying to tell you to feed them what they need to survive in health. Unfortunately, because we are now addicted to our diet, when we sense that hunger, we just reach for the next fast food to satisfy the moment, and the cycle continues in a downward spiral.

This same "instant" religion and "instant" faith has created seed sown along the roadside and in rocky soil. We run from here to there, to this meeting to that, to a one-hour church service to the next. We hear what is said, we shout "Amen!" and we feel good leaving the service or teaching. Yet have we really been nourished? Have we really grasped and understood? Was it something lasting that was provided, or simply a quick fix until the next meeting? How much of what we hear or read just passes us by because we don't take the time to research and meditate on what we heard? We gulp our food down in bite-size chunks instead of chewing on it like a cow chewing on a cud for the purpose of getting the most nutrition possible out of it. And we wonder why we have so many digestive upsets and problems. Proverbs 15:14, in The Message translation, sums it up beautifully: *"An intelligent person is always eager to take in more truth; fools feed on fast-food fads and fancies."*

In Matthew 3:13, Jesus, in speaking of the people said: *"This is the reason I speak to them in parables, because having the power of seeing they do not see, and having the power of hearing they do not hear, nor do they grasp and understand."* Jesus clearly indicates that these people are not blind or deaf. They have the power—the ability—to see and hear, to grasp and to understand; yet they do not. The result of this is in verse 17: *"Truly, I tell you, many prophets and righteous men—men who were upright and in right standing with God—yearned to see what you see, and did not see it, and to hear what you hear, and did not hear it."*

God says in His Word that when the enemy comes in like a flood, He will raise up a standard against that flood. The key, therefore, is discerning the signs of the times and discerning the voice of God in the midst of our circumstances. God did not come to Elijah in a whirlwind or a storm or a fire. He came in a still, small voice, and He still comes that way today. We must be willing to press past the din of the world, press past instantaneous religious satisfaction, and sit quietly and wait at the feet of the Master to find our place in Him and in this world. This calls for an intimate relationship with Him.

The Bible is also clear that satan is the father of lies and deceptive schemes. To everything, there is a reciprocal: north versus south, hot versus cold. Satan takes those things that God creates and means for good and uses them for our destruction. This is one of the reasons why the Bible speaks the reciprocal to satan's lies to us in Romans 8:28: *"We know that all things work together for good to them that love God, to them who are the called according to His purpose."*

The concept of partnership is one of Divine origin—one God, and God alone, imagined, visualized, and created. He made man in His image and likeness and placed man on the earth as a partner with Himself to rule, to reign, and to multiply His Kingdom and His likeness. Satan takes that same concept and uses it for the reciprocal—to multiply his kingdom of death and destruction. Whom we partner with, then, in any aspect of our lives, is critical, because whomever we partner with is what we ourselves will bring into our own lives and reproduce in the lives of those around us. The consequences of our associations will either be a blessing or a curse.

Just as certain actions have certain consequences, so the laws of God are immutable—whether you believe it will or not. If you jump off a building without a parachute, you will fall straight down and hurt yourself or die. If you stick your hand under scalding water, you will burn yourself. If you eat nothing but fat and sugar, you will become fat and sickly. Conversely, if you exercise, eat right, don't smoke, limit alcohol and stress, you will be blessed with better physical health, better mental health, better mobility, and a longer life.

The reality is that the information in this book can greatly benefit both Christians and the secular world equally, because, once again, the laws of God are immutable. In His Word, the Bible, God has laid out many "cause-and-effect" actions that will happen regardless of whether you believe in Him or not, simply because His Word is truth and cannot lie. Let's take the scripture that "you will reap what you sow." God created seedtime and harvest, and He also created seed to reproduce after its own kind (e.g., an orange from an orange) for the purpose of _continuous_ reproduction. He didn't create a seed to produce a hybrid.

Now this is an important thing to know and essential to partnership, because everything that God created in the beginning was good. It is man, through genetic engineering, that has taken something that God created as good, tampered with it, and changed what and how the seed would grow—changed God's original intent, thinking that he could improve on what God created. In manipulating the genetics of the seed, most "natural" seeds now produced are sterile . . . *they are unable to reproduce themselves.* What an insult to our Creator and a contradiction to His initial command by men motivated by lust and greed and inspired by satan himself, working in absolute harmony with them to produce death. This is certainly the reciprocal to God's original intent. God is life!

Putting this in the context of "you will reap what you sow," what happens if you sow a sterile seed? It may produce fruit for you this season but never again. By this action, the blessings of God—of *continuous* provision and multiplication—have been canceled out. Let's look at this logically. If you plant a sterile seed of corn, you will get one plant that will bear two ears. That's it. Even if you plant one of the seeds from one of those kernels, nothing will happen. But what if you plant a perfect seed in good, well tended soil? You get one plant with, let's say, two ears. You take one seed from each ear and replant them. Those two seeds will yield four seeds; then the four seeds will yield eight ears; the eight will yield sixteen . . . it is the power of exponents at work.

This law—God's law—of sowing and reaping works regardless, because it is a spiritual *law*. The same is true of partnership. There are many blessings—spiritual laws and principles—that God sets forth in His Word that are activated when individuals, or businesses for that matter, partner together with His anointed and appointed ministries. If you, therefore, are reading this book but you do not consider yourself a Christian, this book is still for you. And maybe, just maybe, it will answer some questions that you have in regard to God and His plan that you've been wondering about.

There are many examples in the Bible of God using "secular" individuals to bless and prosper those individuals who were working as true ambassadors of Jehovah, three being King Darius and King Cyrus, in the book of Ezra, and King Artaxerxes, in the book of Nehemiah. Matthew 10:40-42 says,

> *He who receives you receives Me, and he who receives Me receives Him who sent Me. He who receives a prophet in the name of a prophet shall receive a prophet's reward. And he who receives a just one in the name of a just one will receive a just one's reward. And whoever shall give to*

one of these little ones a cup of cold water to drink, only in the name of a disciple, truly I say to you, He shall in no way lose his reward.

These verses do not specify that the person "receiving" a man or woman of God have to be a believer in the Lord God to receive the blessing. Matthew 5:45 says that God *"makes His sun to rise on the evil and on the good, and sends rain on the just and on the unjust."* The difference, therefore, is not the blessing, which all will receive—either on earth, in heaven, or both. The difference is the question of your eternal salvation, which you will not receive unless you confess Jesus Christ as Lord and Savior.

God's original intent was (and still is) to financially prosper His people, and there are numerous examples and confirmations in scripture that attest to this. He prospered His people when they first entered the Promised Land, and part of His motivation was to use their prosperity as a drawing factor to encourage heathen nations to trade with His people. Through this process, He gave all heathens the opportunity to meet with Him and, subsequently, to receive salvation. Second Peter 3:9 (GW) confirms this: *"The Lord isn't slow to do what He promised, as some people think. Rather, He is patient for your sake. He doesn't want to destroy anyone **but wants all people to have an opportunity to turn to Him and change the way they think and act.**"* In Romans 6:23 (MKJV), we have another confirmation of this: *"For the wages of sin is death, but the gift of God is eternal life through Jesus Christ our Lord."*

This same principle is still the very quintessence of the Lord's heart—that whosoever shall believe in Jesus Christ shall inherit eternal life with Him (refer to John 6:40). God's people, working together in perfect harmony through the various forms of partnership still hold this desire—and potential—within their grasp. Partnership with the Lord first and then with one another, to promote His Kingdom and promise of eternal life, crosses all dividing lines, destroys all barriers, and is the single most powerful tool of unification.

As followers and believers of the Lord Jesus Christ, we should understand that our first and foremost allegiance is to Him and His kingdom. Even in theological disagreements amongst ourselves, we should display this one unification factor of unity. Our complete commitment to Him and to one another should stand as a testimony and an example to unbelievers. It should promote His kingdom, His virtues, and the gift of eternal life to whosoever will believe.

The Constitution of the United States of America is that one binding element that holds the citizens together in complete unity. The Constitution starts with the preamble: "We the people." How much more should the Christian church today not be the original mirror from which the Constitution is reflected?

"We the people—God's people . . ."

Izak Bester

Chapter 1

PARTNERSHIP DEFINED

Two are better than one; because they have a good reward for their labor.
For if they fall, the one will lift up his fellow; but woe to him who is
alone when he falls, for he does not have another to help him. Again,
if two lie together, then they have warmth; but how can one be warm
alone? And if one overthrows him, two shall withstand him; and a
threefold cord is not quickly broken. (Eccles. 4:9-12 MKJV)

Partnership with man, partnership with all of His creation, and partnership between all men is an all-encompassing ordinance of God that was introduced at creation and continues unbroken in the New Testament. In fact, the principles of partnership saturate the entire Bible.

We first read of God's intentions regarding partnership in Genesis 2:18 when He said:

"*It is not good for the man to be alone.*
*I will make a **companion** who will help him.*" (NLT)
"*I will make him an **help** meet for him.*" (KJV)
"*I will make him a **helper** comparable to him.*" (NKJV)
"*I'll make him a **helper**, a **companion**.*" (MSG)

*"I will make him a **helper** meet (suitable, adapted, completing) for him." (AMPL)*

In the original Aramaic text, the word used for *help* as we find it in the King James translation of Genesis 2:18 is *azar*—pronounced "aw-zar"—which means "to surround, that is, protect or aid: help, succour." This word appears twenty-one times in the Old Testament and is used in the context of protecting, aiding, or helping another person. Moses, speaking to the Israelites in Deuteronomy 33:29 says, *"Happy art thou, O Israel: who is like unto thee, O people saved by the LORD, **the shield of thy help**, and who is the sword of thy excellency! and thine enemies shall be found liars unto thee; and thou shalt tread upon their high places."*

Joshua, during the time of entering and possessing the Promised Land, spoke to three of the tribes of Israel after Moses' death in Joshua 1:14, saying: *"Your wives, your little ones, and your cattle shall remain in the land which Moses gave you on this side Jordan. But you shall go armed before your brothers, all the mighty men of valor, and **help them** until Jehovah has given your brothers rest."*

In 1 Chronicles 12:17, when David was in Ziklag, there were men from Benjamin and Judah who came to him. David said to them: *"If you have come to me in peace, to **help** me, my heart shall be knit to you."* They answered, saying: *"We are yours, David, and on your side, son of Jesse."* More and more men came to surround, protect, and aid David as indicated in verse 22: *"For at that time they came to David day by day to **help** him, until it was a great army, like an army of God."* By these scriptures, we can see that the principle of a helper, a partner, is of Divine origin.

When God said: *"I will make him a **helper** meet (suitable, adapted, completing) for him,"* it was again confirmation of His Divine intent as regards partnership. The purpose for creating Eve was primarily to surround, protect, and aid Adam. When God created Eve, he took a part of Adam, specifically a rib from Adam's body. A rib surrounds and protects the vital organs—the lungs and heart. The ribs, along with the muscles of the chest, also aid in breathing. God was displaying that partnership, as designed and created by Him, is essential to life itself. He also noted that there was nothing in all creation that could surround, protect, or aid Adam as only Eve could. Our Creator has never had the intention that

20

each person should be completely independent of another. From the very start—from Adam and Eve—the Lord instituted the principles of partnership and colaboring, one with another.

The famous poet John Donne, a deeply religious man and often called the founder of the Metaphysical Poets, wrote some very inspiring articles on the coexistence of mankind from a biblical perspective. He wrote a series of prayers called *Devotions upon Emergent Occasions*. These came during his later years, and they reflect a spiritual perception of the essential oneness of life. In these devotions, he made a profound statement. He said: "No man is an island, entire of itself; every man is a piece of the continent, a part of the main."

The word *genesis* means "the act of producing," or "a new beginning." Inherent within every life form, within every seed, is the Divine desire and contained potential for continual reproduction. This is because God—the only Creator—is the source of all life, and all of creation ultimately points to Him. Man is no different. In Genesis 1:26 (MKJV), we read: "*And God said, Let Us make man in Our image, after Our likeness. And let them have dominion over the fish of the sea, and over the fowl of the heavens, and over the cattle, and over all the earth, and over all the creepers creeping on the earth.*"

Man was created to represent God on this earth with certain same inherent qualities and abilities as Himself in order to oversee all of created life. The Message translation quotes verse 27 as follows: "*God created human beings; He created them godlike, reflecting God's nature. He created them male and female.*" Then in Genesis 1:28, we read: "*And God blessed them. And God said to them, Be fruitful, and multiply and fill the earth, and subdue it. And have dominion over the fish of the sea and over the fowl of the heavens, and all animals that move upon the earth.*"

It was God's original design for man and woman to come together in partnership, in covenant, for the purposes of reproduction. When He created Adam, He formed him from the dust of the earth. Dust is a loose substance, just like sand. Dust by itself cannot hold shape but needs a binding agent to bring and hold it together as a solid substance. So man, with the absolute wisdom of God, was created for partnership and with the need for partnership. Man was dead, not a living thing—in the earth, of the earth. Then God blew His breath—life—(breath consisting of water and DNA) into Him. Water was the "partner" that turned dust into a solid substance. He made Himself part of Adam, and He made Adam part of Himself, because His intentions were to partner with man, and therefore man should be made worthy to partner with Him. The only way to accomplish that was to make the human race—Adam—acceptable to His presence. Genesis 5:1 (MKJV) says, *"In the day God created man, **He made him in the likeness of God**."* None of the rest of His creation was created in this same manner. He gave Himself with the sole intent of creating a (human) being in His image, and as a consequence, man then possessed the same potential to continue with the process.

In Genesis 8:22, the Lord continues with the principles of partnership by establishing the law of sowing and reaping. The soil cannot produce without the seed, nor can the seed produce without the soil. Both the soil and the seed need to come together (partner together) to accomplish their common purpose, i.e., to produce fruit, and when the fruit comes, many are those who enjoy it. The contained potential in each individual seed is not only to produce one little fruit but also abundant fruit filled with more abundant seed that can feed and sustain many, and to produce a method for the continuation of provision through the sowing again of part of the harvest.

In addition, when a farmer sees a good tree, he will take special care of both tree and soil to ensure a good harvest every season. It is not only a large harvest that is important but also the quality in taste and nutrition of what is produced. A farmer is known for the fruit from his land. It is known that people will come from far to enjoy the fruit of a good tree when they have tasted its goodness and, most assuredly, will they also tell others. Just so, it is for the glory of the Lord God when we are able to unite together and work together with the common purpose of expanding His Kingdom by the good fruit we produce. It gives Him great delight when He is recognized in and by this world through the unified and combined fruit-producing actions of His children. Again, although each has a different function in the production of the fruit, it is the combined action of the soil, the seed, God's blessing, and the farmer that brings forth the biggest and the best harvest possible.

What exactly is *partnership* **or a** *partner* **or a** *helper*? Let us start with the word *helper*. We have said that according to *Strong's Dictionary,* the Hebrew word for *help* and *helper* means "to surround; i.e., to protect or aid; help."

The *Webster's Dictionary* defines *help* as:

1. To aid; to assist; to lend strength or means toward effecting a purpose.
2. To help a man in his work; to help another in raising a building.
3. To help forward, to advance by assistance.
4. To help on, to forward; to promote by aid.
5. To help to, to supply with; to furnish with.
6. That which gives assistance; he or that which contributes to advance a purpose.
7. To lend aid; to contribute strength or means.

The *Encarta World English Dictionary* defines *help* as:

1. Assist somebody: to make it easier or possible for somebody to do something that one person cannot do alone by providing assistance.
2. Advise somebody: to provide somebody with advice, directions, or other information.
3. Provide for somebody's needs: to provide somebody with something that he or she needs.
4. Advance something: to promote the advancement or improvement of something.

If we put all this together, we can see in all these definitions the overriding theme of one person contributing strength, support, and supplies to another for the purpose of improving, building, and advancing. If we truly understand this, **_all_** of us—every single believer in Jesus Christ—would forever be promoting our neighbor and our fellow believers and not ourselves; we would understand in doing so we ourselves would also be assisted and promoted in whatever we are doing. This is Kingdom mentality: promoting, surrounding, helping, aiding, and assisting others who are promoting the Kingdom. It is God's law of sowing and reaping in action.

Now let's look at the word *partner* and *partnership*. We can look to Luke 5:9-10 for an example. The term *partner* is used here to describe a working relationship between the fishermen James, John, and Simon. The Greek translation of partner is *koinonos*, which means, "a sharer, that is, associate, companion, fellowship, partaker, partner." In 2 Corinthians 8:23, Paul uses this same Greek word to describe Titus as a "partner and fellow worker." Interestingly enough, the Greek word we know as *koinonia* comes from the same word used here for partner. *Koinonia* is used within the Christian church to describe the coming together of believers for fellowship. It is defined as "partnership; participation; social intercourse; benefaction; to communicate; to contribute; distribution; fellowship."

From a secular viewpoint, the *Oxford Dictionary* defines *partnership* as "a joint venture, to team up with, to connect with, to join, to collaborate." It defines *partner* as "a person who shares and takes part with another in a joint venture, to affiliate with. A co-worker."

The *Encarta World English Dictionary* defines *partnership* as:

1. The relationship between two or more people or organizations that are involved in the same activity.
2. Cooperation between people or groups working together.
3. Group of people working together: an organization formed by two or more people or groups who work together for some purpose.

It defines a *partner* as "somebody who shares activity: somebody who is involved in an activity with somebody else."

It is evident by looking at all these definitions that the root meanings of the words *helper* and *partner*, as we find in Genesis 2:18, essentially serve the same purpose and certainly convey the same meaning and intentions. We can also think of partner(ship) in terms of an actual ship. Think about a ship out in the middle of the ocean, away from land. All workers on board that ship must be working together to properly steer and navigate the ship in order to shelter, protect and provide for the passengers on board. Everyone has a task to do—a "job assignment." Even though the workers are doing different tasks, each task is essential to moving the ship forward in a positive manner for the benefit of all aboard. So it is with partnership within the ministry: to not only provide for the "staff" (those who are saved) but also the "guests" (those who may not be saved). Second Corinthians 2:14-15 reads: *"Now thanks be to God who always leads us in triumph in Christ, and through us diffuses the fragrance of His knowledge in every place. For we are to God the fragrance of Christ among those who are being saved and those who are perishing."*

In the light of all the above definitions and explanations, we can define partner(ship) as an agreement between two or more persons to collaborate, to team up, to join and work together toward a common purpose in a joint venture, and to unify and combine all abilities and resources in order to accomplish that purpose. Partnership is also companionship, friendship and camaraderie, with the intent of surrounding one another for the mutual benefit of aiding and protecting one another.

The concept of partnership is shown clearly even within the human body, in how one part of the body is dependent upon all the other parts. The principle of colaboring one with another is seen in almost every single body process that takes place—from seeing to hearing, to digesting food, to protection from sickness and disease, etc. If all body cells, tissues and organs are functioning in perfect harmony and productivity, the health and ability of the body as a whole increases. So it is with the corporate body of Christ. The health of all increases the resources and abilities (as well as the ability to do more with less, becoming more efficient), while the neglect of even one body part will decrease resources and productivity.

Partnership is a system designed and initiated by God from the very foundations of His creation, and His every intention behind it is for our individual and mutual benefit. The very basis of nature, of humanity, of the universe, was created with covenant partnership and reproduction on the mind of our Lord God—Creator of all. His objective for partnership is to continue with the process of reproduction and to provide a means of increasing the resources, abilities, rewards, protection, and provision for the body of Christ as a whole and for every believer individually—far beyond our wildest expectations.

Chapter 2

CO-WORKERS WITH THE LORD
OF THE HARVEST

When the Lord Jesus started His ministry here on earth, He exemplified this same ordinance of partnership. The very first thing He did was to call to Himself disciples (partners) who would help Him to accomplish His Divine purposes (Matt. 4:18-22). Those partners were not only called to help but were also equipped to continue with His message of salvation throughout all the ages to come. Christianity and the Christian Church today is a direct result of the fruits of those initial partnerships.

In Mark 4:30-32, the Lord Jesus again confirms this principle as being part of the New Covenant when He likened the Kingdom of God to a mustard seed. The mustard seed by itself is a very small seed. Yet when it was "partnered" with good soil, it grew up to become a great herb tree, providing a place of shelter and rest for "others," represented by the birds. This is the foundational understanding of the purpose of ministries and the storehouse concept: We are to partner together in order to provide for each other and also for others in need. In doing so, we provide a place where "birds" can "nest" under our "shade," or protection. And when birds nest, they reproduce, creating an increase in the harvest and blessing of family. When the offspring leave the nest, they take some of the seeds with them, which in turn get sown elsewhere, increasing the harvest and blessing even further. It is this law of relationship based on sowing and reaping that is so important to God.

Let's read 1 Peter 2:9 (AMPL): *"But **you are a chosen race, a royal priesthood, a dedicated nation**, (God's) own purchased, special people, that you may set forth the wonderful deeds and display the virtues and perfections of Him Who called you out of darkness into His marvelous light."*

Did you notice this verse of scripture says, *"a chosen race, a royal priesthood, a dedicated nation"*? That means God considers us as *His chosen people*—chosen to further His original intention of partnership as defined in Genesis 2:18. This verse speaks of a very specific Divine Commission and mandate given to each and every believer. We, the body of Christ, both individually and corporately, have been chosen, elected, appointed, equipped, and enabled to become His co-workers upon this earth! As with everything else in God's creation, there is a Divine purpose behind this. What is the purpose? We find the answer in the second half of 1 Peter 2:9: *"**That you may set forth the wonderful deeds and display the virtues and perfections of Him . . .**"*

So what does it mean in every day language? It means we—His royal priesthood—are His chosen and dedicated ones who have the Divine Commission to bring forth into manifestation and demonstrate, promote, publish, and communicate the wonderful deeds, the intrinsic values, and perfections of God Almighty into this world. I would say that epitomizes partnership with God and man in every possible definition available. We are called to, as the Bible says, "diffuse the fragrance of Christ" in to the world, to be ambassadors sent by God to represent and display Jesus and His Kingdom to the kingdoms on and of the earth. Second Corinthians 5:20 (MKJV) says, *"Then we are ambassadors on behalf of Christ, as God exhorting through us, we beseech you on behalf of Christ, be reconciled to God."* The Message translation of 2 Corinthians 5:20 says it this way: *"We're Christ's representatives. God uses us to persuade men and women to drop their differences and enter into God's work of making things right between them. We're speaking for Christ Himself now: Become friends with God; He's already a friend with you."*

To fully understand the context of what the Apostle Paul was saying, we must understand what an Ambassador or a Representative is to begin with. The *Encarta World English Dictionary* defines *ambassador* as a "diplomatic representative: a diplomatic official of the highest rank sent by one country as its long-term representative to another" and "official representative: an official representative of an organization or movement."

The *American Heritage Dictionary* has a slightly broader definition: "a diplomatic official of the highest rank appointed and accredited as representative in residence by one government or sovereign to another, usually for a specific length of time."

The *Encarta World English Dictionary* defines a *representative* as "somebody who speaks for others: somebody who speaks, acts, or votes on behalf of others" and "member of legislature: a member of a legislative assembly."

An ambassador, therefore, is a person that is approved, certified, qualified, recognized, and endorsed by a government or organization to represent the fellow citizens and the interests of the government or organization in foreign lands. They are expected to promote the rights, the values, and the principles of their nation, as well as to protect and promote the welfare of their people residing in the foreign land. In addition, they are to promote their culture within the foreign land and protect their core values and interests abroad. Should a situation arise deeming so, they are to initiate legal proceedings on behalf of their country and defend lawsuits initiated against it.

As ambassadors on behalf of Jesus Christ, who is the King of Heaven and whom we as Christians represent, we are to do these exact same things. Ephesians 2:19 says that when we become reconciled to God through the sanctifying blood of Christ Jesus, we are no longer foreigners or strangers within His land. We become citizens of the household of the God of the Universe and therefore partners with Him for the purpose of promoting and protecting His Kingdom.

We as Christians must understand what happens when we choose to become Christians. It seems sometimes either we have forgotten the following or never had it explained to us to begin with. Jesus commanded us to be *in* the world but not *of* the world. Jesus also said that His Kingdom is not of this world, and unless we are "born again," we cannot enter His Kingdom—Heaven. In other words, we cannot become citizens of Heaven, nor can we be ambassadors for Him, or partake in the benefits of citizenship with Him. When we were born, we were physically born into this world—not His. By default, wherever our parents lived at the time of our birth is where we became citizens. When we hear the gospel and we choose—by an act of our will, not by force or coercion but out of understanding who Christ Jesus is—we also choose to become a citizen of Heaven. When we become "born again," with our parent being God the Father and the Holy Spirit, our citizenship now becomes where He is from: Heaven. This citizenship and the allegiance that comes with that citizenship now supersede *any* earthly citizenship and worldly allegiance we have.

By all the above definitions, we can see that the words *partner* and *helper* as defined in Genesis Chapter One and *ambassador* and *representative* defined here all have the same root meaning. If we are partners with God first and then with each other in the context of promoting the spreading of the Gospel of the Lord Jesus, it means we are co-laborers and co-workers with God by definition. It is also impossible to be the ambassador of two countries at once. We as His ambassadors are to promote the rights, the values, and the principles of our Heavenly citizenship into an unbelieving world as we function, first and foremost, as co-workers with the Lord in order to spread the good news of His saving grace through the Lord Jesus Christ. God is clear in His word: you cannot serve two masters. You will either love one and hate the other, or hate one and love the other. The values of the world's systems, ungodly governments, and societies are not ruled by God and, therefore, are in direct opposition to God.

As Christians, we are not ambassadors on behalf of this world to God or to any other country. We are not to promote worldly values within the Embassy of Heaven.

Every foreign government has an Embassy where the Ambassador lives and where his or her culture is prevalent. For believers, this is the church and Christ-centered ministries. How we are to act within this culture is well defined in 2 Corinthians 6:1 (MKJV): "*But **working together**, we also call on you not to receive the grace of God in vain*." The Greek word used here to emphasize the essence of "working together" is *sunergeo*, which means "to be a fellow worker, that is, cooperate: help (work) with, work(er) together." The Amplified Bible puts it this way: "***As God's fellow workers laboring together with Him***."

We are called, as ambassadors and as fellow citizens, with the Kingdom of God being our primary place of citizenship, to work together, to partner together, to labor together with Jesus Christ and with each other for the advancement of His Kingdom wherever we go and with whomever we meet. The Apostle Paul wrote in 1 Corinthians 3:6-9 (BBE) about this same concept of partnership and being fellow workers with God: "*I did the planting, Apollos did the watering, but God gave the increase. So then the planter is nothing, and the waterer is nothing; but God who gives the increase. **Now the planter and the waterer are working for the same end: but they will have their separate rewards in the measure of their work**.*"

In an exposition of 1 Corinthians 3:6-9, the *Barnes' Commentary* has the following to say:

> For we are laborers together with God. We are God's co-workers. A similar expression occurs in 2 Corinthians 6:1, 'We then as workers together with Him,' etc. This passage is capable of two significations: first, as in our translation, that they were co-workers with God; engaged with Him in His work, that He and they cooperated in the production of the effect; or that it was a joint-work; as we speak of a partnercy, or of joint-effort among people . . . If this is the idea, it gives a special sacredness to the work of the ministry, and indeed to the work of the farmer and the vinedresser. There is no higher honor than for a man to be engaged in doing the same things which God does, and participating with Him in accomplishing His glorious plans.

We are to understand that as co-workers with the Lord, we should adopt—by the renewing of our minds—*His* mindset. Remember in Genesis 1:27, we learned that God created man "***Godlike, reflecting***

God's nature." This renewing of the mind speaks about reclaiming that original intent through our thinking processes in opposition to worldly training and subsequent values. When we partner with Him, His priorities should become our priorities. Through this process of renewing of our minds, we will discover and accomplish His purpose for our existence. Proverbs 16:3 (AMPL) puts this in wonderful perspective: "*Roll your works upon the Lord—commit and trust them wholly to Him. He will cause your thoughts to become agreeable to His will, and so shall your plans be established.*"

When we partner with the Lord, when we make His works and His purposes first priority in our own lives, then He Himself will see to it that our plans will become infused with His will and purposes, with the added benefit of us walking in the fullness of His very personal involvement in every area of our lives. This is a guaranteed guarantee of success for us all! His purposes stand far above our level of expectancy. By making His priorities become our priorities we are elevated far above our own levels of expectancy, far above the limitations of worldly thinking, and we will start to operate within the manifestation of His Divine abilities as a matter of course.

The concept of partnership with the Lord Jesus and His appointed ministries is not new. As we've seen above and will continue to see, it saturates the pages of the Bible. However, as with many other blessings the Lord has given us, we can only come to the full understanding of the hidden treasures waiting for us as we submit our will and purposes to the Lord. This understanding—this revelation—will only come about when we are willing to understand, through the renewal of our minds, *His* Divine intentions. The renewing of our minds comes through daily adoption and submission to the tenants of the faith taught by Jesus Christ in the completeness of His Word and through the revelation of that word through the teaching of the Holy Spirit within us. As Christians, we are *in* the world but not *of* the world.

In John 18:36, Jesus declares that His Kingdom is not of this world. In John 17:16, Jesus is praying for all believers when He says, "*They are not of the world, even as I am not of the world.*" When we become born again believers in the Lord Jesus Christ, our spirits are reborn into the Kingdom of God and we are awarded and we accept our primary citizenship within that Kingdom. There then starts a transition time where our born again spirit is of God, but our flesh is still of the world we have been walking in. In this beginning, our flesh and its carnal desires rule over the spirit and, therefore, our values—those things we act out and represent to others—are still dictated by what the world says. The process of renewing our minds is saying no to the flesh and letting the spirit lead. It is only in this process of partnering with and colaboring with the Holy Spirit that we begin to manifest God's rule and authority, first in our own lives, then within the church and the ministries we represent, and finally the world.

In view of the various definitions and expositions of partnership we have seen above, Romans 12:2-10, in The Message translation, is giving us one of the best perspectives of partnership that is the result of the process of renewed mindsets and conforming to God's definition of the purposes of partnership:

> *Don't become so well-adjusted to your culture that you fit into it without even thinking. Instead, fix your attention on God. You'll be changed from the inside out. Readily recognize what He wants from you, and quickly respond to it. Unlike the culture around you, always dragging you down to its level of immaturity, God brings the best out of you, develops well-formed maturity in you. I'm speaking to you out of deep gratitude for all that God has given me, and especially as I have responsibilities in relation to you. Living then, as every one of you does, in pure grace, it's important that you not misinterpret yourselves as people who are bringing this goodness to God. No, God brings it all to you.*

We find one of the most perfect models of partnership displayed in the human body—created in the image and likeness of God. Partnership is like the various parts of the body, with each part getting its meaning from the various other parts and then from the body as a whole, not the other way around. As believers, we all—as various parts—make up Christ's body, and each of us find our individual meaning and function as a part of His body. If we were a chopped-off finger or cut-off toe, we wouldn't amount to much, would we? So since we find ourselves fashioned into all these excellently formed and marvelously functioning parts in Christ's body, let us take decisive steps to partner first with the Lord and His works, then with one another in His body—the church and His appointed ministries.

In John 1:3-4 (ISV) the Apostle John in explaining the Divine nature of the Lord Jesus Christ says, "*Through Him all things were made, and apart from Him nothing was made that has been made. In Him was life, and that life brought light to humanity.*" Colossians 1:16-17 (AMPL) continues to say: "*For it was in Him that all things were created, in heaven and on earth, things seen and things unseen, whether thrones, dominions, rulers or authorities; all things were created and exist through Him (by His service, intervention) and in and for Him. And He Himself existed before all things and in Him all things consist—cohere, are held together.*" Only within the Lord Jesus Christ do we find the fullness of the body in its most perfect form. Anything outside of that body is not part of that body. We, the body of Christ here on earth, have been created in, through, for, and by Jesus Christ, and the key to understanding the reason for our existence lies in discovering first of all HIS purpose for us. The only accurate way to understand ourselves is by who God is and by what He does for us, not by what we are and what we do for Him.

This principle of unity in purpose amongst His children and the Lord's Divine intentions regarding this unity is very clearly depicted in His prayer just before His arrest and crucifixion:

> *I pray for them. I do not pray for the world, but for those whom You have given Me, for they are Yours. And I do not pray for these alone, **but for those also who shall believe on Me through their word, that they all may be one, as You, Father, are in Me, and I in You, that they also may be one in Us, so that the world may believe that You have sent Me. And I have given them the glory which You have given Me, that they may be one, even as We are one, I in them, and You in Me, that they may be made perfect in one;** and that the world may know that You have sent Me*

33

and have loved them as You have loved Me. (John 17:9, 20-23 MKJV)

In the God's Word Translation, verse 23 says,

> *I am in them, and You are in Me.* **So they are completely united.** *In this way the world knows that You have sent Me and that You have loved them in the same way You have loved Me.*

We are to become completely united in our faith in Jesus Christ as Lord and Savior, and then we are to become completely united in our efforts to proclaim Him as Savior and Lord. It is only through united effort as partners—first with Him and then, as a continuation, amongst ourselves—operating as one body with one common goal, one common purpose: that His Kingdom will advance as the mighty army we are called and destined to be.

It is all about coming into unity through partnership—first, with God and, second, with one another. God never intended for us to be alone—operating on our own. He also did not intend for us to be separate but to be operating as a whole. For example, two men or two women may be together, but they are still separate. God separated woman from man, and it is only when a man and a woman come together in the way God intended it that a whole is made. The definition of *unity* is "the condition of being in agreement, harmony." *Harmony* is defined as "agreement in ideas, feelings, etc. The sounding together in a way that is pleasing to hear." Matthew 18:19 (AMPL) says, *"Again I tell you, if two of you on earth agree (harmonize together, together make a symphony) about—anything and everything—whatever they shall ask, it will come to pass and be done for them by My Father in heaven."* It is only when we come together in agreement with each other and God that the house is strengthened and prospers.

It is inherent within the design of covenant partnership that we all be dependent on one another to cause a synergistic effect. Synergy is when two substances are combined, and the combined action is greater than either of the individual actions by themselves. It is really simple multiplication: $2 \times 2 = 4$, $4 \times 4 = 16$, $16 \times 16 = 256$, etc. In Genesis 1:22, God gives the command to Adam and Eve to be fruitful and multiply—not add. In Genesis 9:1 and 9:7, God gives the same command to Noah, his family, and all creatures with them. In Ezekiel 36:10-11, 30 God, in speaking to the mountains continues with the same multiplication in mind:

> *And I will multiply men on you, all the house of Israel, all of it. And the cities shall have people, and the wastes shall be built. And I will multiply men and beast on you, and they shall increase and be fruitful. And I will make you dwell as before, and I will do better to you than at your beginnings. And you shall know that I am Jehovah. And I will multiply the fruits of the tree and the increase of the field, so that you shall never again receive the curse of famine among the nations.*

To multiply means an exponential increase of much more than a simple addition. The very nature of God speaks of multiplication and our agreement through partnership—first, with Him and then, as a continuation, with one another—is the activator for the manifestation of His multiplication promises.

The *Barnes' Commentary* on John 17:23 has the following to say:

> **May be made perfect in one**—That their union may be complete. That there may be no jars, discords, or contentions. A machine is perfect or complete when it has all its parts and is in good order when there is no portion of it wanting. So the union of Christians, for which the Savior prayed, would be complete or perfect if there were no controversies, no envying, no contentions, and no heart-burnings and jealousies. It is worthy of remark here how entirely the union of His people occupied the mind of Jesus as He drew near to death. He saw the danger of strife and contentions in the church. He knew the imperfections of even the best of men. He saw how prone they would be to passion and ambition; how ready to mistake love of sect or party for zeal for pure religion; how selfish and worldly men in the church might divide

His followers, and produce unholy feeling and contention; and He saw, also, how much this would do to dishonor religion. Hence, He took occasion, when He was about to die, to impress the importance of union on His disciples. By solemn admonition, and by most tender and affecting appeals to God in supplication, He showed his sense of the value of this union. He used the most sublime and impressive illustration; He adverted to the eternal union between the Father and Himself; He reminded them of His love, and of the effect that their union would have on the world, to fix it more deeply in their hearts. The effect has shown the infinite wisdom of the Savior. The contentions and strife of Christians have shown His knowledge in foreseeing it. The effect of all this on religion has shown that He understood the value of union. Christians have contended long enough. It is time that they should hear the parting admonitions of their Redeemer, and go united against their common foe.

John 17:20-23 clearly depicts God's intentions of partnership and we being co-workers with Him. The Lord Jesus Christ is called the "Son of Man" because He represents the Lord's every intention for His original creation of man—Adam. The Lord Jesus Christ is also called the "Second Adam" because He is the perfection of the fullness of God's original intention for mankind—the intention and abilities coupled with the Divine Commission to "take dominion." Found within Him, we are endowed and empowered to function as a whole and continue with the Divine Commission as we work together in unity.

In Isaiah 49:6 (MSG), the Lord, speaking about the Lord Jesus, says, *"But that's not a big enough job for my servant—just to recover the tribes of Jacob, merely to round up the strays of Israel. **I'm setting you up as a light for the nations so that my salvation becomes global!**"* In Matthew 28:18-20 (MKJV), the Lord Jesus then gave His followers His mandate to continue with the same work He came to do when He said: *"**All authority is given to Me in Heaven and in earth. Therefore go and teach all nations**, baptizing them in the name of the Father and of the Son and of the Holy Spirit, teaching them to observe all things, whatever I commanded you. And, behold, I am with you all the days until the end of* *the world. Amen.*" The Message translation quotes verses 18 and 19 this way: "**God authorized and commanded me to commission you**: *Go out and train everyone you meet, far and near, in this way of life, marking them by baptism in the threefold name: Father, Son, and Holy Spirit.*" So here we again see the commission to become His ambassadors. Remember the definition "an official representative of an organization or movement." We are ALL called, commanded, and commissioned by the Lord to make disciples for Him. All means ALL, and that means NOBODY is left out. However, we all have to work together, just as was the case with the first disciples. The Lord Jesus underlined this very important aspect when He sent His Disciples ahead of Him—instructing them to go out in pairs of two: "*And He called the Twelve and began to send them out **by two and two**. And He gave them authority over unclean spirits*" (Mark 6:7).

The principle is this: we are to partner with the Lord first, and then we are to partner with each other as a continuation of that same relationship we have with Him, being one with Him as He is one with the Father. Partnering with the Lord means exactly what we read in Colossians 1:10 (MSG): "*We pray that you'll live well for the Master, making Him proud of you as you work hard in His orchard. As you learn more and more how God works, you will learn how to do your work.*" Partnership with one another in terms of this commission is to enter into an agreement to promote the work of the Lord on this earth. Partnering with the Lord in promoting His work means doing whatever, wherever He directs. Our interpartnership with one another should have this fundamental objective as the very foundation upon which it is built. This foundation—of which the Lord Jesus Christ is the cornerstone—is what should become our primary focus and, subsequently, should energize us as both individuals as well as Christian communities to leave no stone untouched but to pursue every possible avenue to fulfill our commission, either directly or indirectly.

We all, individually and as Christian communities, have been given tasks to perform in the fulfillment of the Great Commission. Mark 13:34 (GW) says, "*It is like a man who went on a trip. As he left home, he put his servants in charge. He assigned work to each one and ordered the guard to be alert.*" Jesus has returned to heaven but is coming back again. In the meantime, He has put His servants—His children—in charge of the greatest project known to mankind and assigned each individual a task to do, a part to play in the development and implementation of the project. How do we know or understand our task or our part? By uniting in partnership: first with the Lord Jesus and then with each other. We discover who we are by discovering who Jesus is, because we are called to be like Jesus. It is in the community together, in *koinonia*, that our individual gifts and talents are often discovered. Iron sharpens iron, and we need each other to nurture and even reveal the hidden things the Holy Spirit has implanted within us for the purpose of community. God has a contribution—many contributions—that He has intended for each and every person to make. If we miss these contributions to His project because we are too busy "doing our own thing," we will subsequently one day have to give an account before God and all the witnesses of heaven of the ruined, empty, or limited harvest we as His servants produced.

In Matthew 25:14-30, we find the parable of a man going away on a journey and entrusting each one of his servants with talents, each according to their individual ability. Upon his return, he called his servants to bring an account as to how they managed those talents he entrusted them with. The servant who initially received the least did nothing with what he was given and was subsequently thrown out of the master's household. No matter what talent we have been given, we are expected to work with it and if possible increase what the Lord has given us. Should we not, then even that which we think we have shall be taken away from us. Conversely, in the same parable we also learn of the increase given to the servant who worked with and increased the talents the most. We are called upon to be faithful stewards, and if we are, we have a promise from God to increase our resources. Matthew 24:45-46 (GW) affirms exactly this: "*Who, then, is the faithful and wise servant? The master will put that person in charge of giving the other servants their food at the right time. That servant will be blessed if his master finds him doing this job when he comes.*"

We see this principle and the subsequent results at work in Acts, chapter 4, when the believers joined together in purpose and resources, and their numbers grew by the thousands daily, so that the Word subsequently went throughout all the earth. All this was for the glory of the Lord.

> *The whole congregation of believers was united as one—one heart, one mind! They didn't even claim*

ownership of their own possessions. No one said, 'That's mine; you can't have it.' They shared everything. The apostles gave powerful witness to the resurrection of the Master Jesus, and grace was on all of them. And so it turned out that not a person among them was needy. Those who owned fields or houses sold them and brought the price of the sale to the apostles and made an offering of it. The apostles then distributed it according to each person's need. (Acts 4:32-35 MSG)

The great Bible scholar Matthew Henry, in his commentary on Acts 4:32, says,

> They were all of one heart, and of one soul. Though there were many, very many, of different ages, tempers, and conditions, in the world, who perhaps, before they believed, were perfect strangers to one another, yet, when they met in Christ, they were as intimately acquainted as if they had known one another many years. Perhaps they had been of different sects among the Jews, before their conversion, or had had discords upon civil accounts; but now these were all forgotten and laid aside, and they were unanimous in the faith of Christ, and, being all joined to the Lord, they were joined to one another in holy love. This was the blessed fruit of Christ's dying precept to his disciples, to love one another, and his dying prayer for them, that they all might be one. We have reason to think they divided themselves into several congregations, or worshipping assemblies, according as their dwellings were, under their respective ministers; and yet this occasioned no jealousy or uneasiness; for they were all of one heart, and one soul, notwithstanding; and loved those of other congregations as truly as those of their own. Thus it was then, and we may not despair of seeing it so again, when the Spirit shall be poured out upon us from on high.

Chapter 3

THE MULTIPLICATION FACTOR

It is our partnership with the Lord that compels us to partner with others in His body in order to produce fruits of Kingdom proportions. Our love for the Lord and our confession of Jesus Christ as Lord is the unification factor that will enjoin us with one heart and one purpose. Remember: Partner(ship) is an agreement between two or more persons to collaborate, to team up, to join and work together toward a common purpose in a joint venture, and to unify and combine all abilities and resources in order to accomplish that purpose. Partnership is also companionship, friendship, and camaraderie, with the intent of surrounding one another for mutual benefit of aiding and protecting one another.

It would be sufficiently satisfying if the reward we received from our partnership in God's work were strictly a heavenly reward waiting for us in eternity. But praise God, it's not! As we shall see in the next chapter about the widow of Zarephath, there's also an earthly aspect to this reward system. Partnership is one of God's ways of providing for us, here and now, blessings and provisions so great we could never muster up enough faith to receive them on our own. 1 Corinthians 2:9 (GW) says, *"But as Scripture says: 'No eye has seen, no ear has heard, and* no mind has imagined the things that God has prepared for those who love Him.'"

Jeremiah 32:37-42 (MKJV) says,

> *Behold, I will gather them out of all countries, whither I have driven them in mine anger, and in my fury, and in great wrath; and I will bring them again unto this place, and I will cause them to dwell safely: And they shall be my people, and I will be their God:* ***And I will give them one heart, and one way, that they may fear me for ever, for the good of them, and of their children after them****: **And I will make an everlasting covenant with them, that I will not turn away from them, to do them good***; but I will put my fear in their hearts, that they shall not depart from me. **Yea, I will rejoice over them to do them good**, and I will plant them in this land assuredly with my whole heart and with my whole soul. For thus saith the LORD; Like as I have brought all this great evil upon this people, **so will I bring upon them all the good that I have promised them**.*

In 1 Peter 3:8-9 (GW), we have a continuation from the Old Testament to the New of this covenantal promise from the Lord. He made us another promise of provision when we are obedient to this command of partnership with each other: "*Finally, everyone must live in harmony, be sympathetic, love each other, have compassion, and be humble. Don't pay people back with evil for the evil they do to you, or ridicule those who ridicule you. Instead, bless them, **because you were called to inherit a blessing**.*" The promise of provision is contained within the phrase "you are called to inherit a blessing."

Who is it that inherits something? It is an heir. When we come into covenant relationship with Jesus Christ, we become sons and daughters of the King of the Universe and, therefore, heirs to what is contained within His Domain. Galatians 3:26, 29 (NIV) says, "*You are all sons of God through faith in Christ Jesus. If you belong to Christ, then you are Abraham's seed and heirs according to the promise.*" The inheritance and the blessing, therefore, are totally based on covenant relationship with Christ, which by its intrinsic nature, extends to relationship with the entire family of God. Within this verse, there is no favoritism: _all_ of God's children—_all_ His heirs—are called to equal inheritance. It is this understanding that should be the catalyst for us joining together in partnership with each other for the purpose of expanding His glorious Kingdom amongst all peoples and tribes across this earth.

Within this, however, we must understand the conditions of inheritance. We have established that it is the heir—the son or daughter—who is eligible to receive the inheritance. When does actual "transfer" come? Galatians 4:1-2, 4 (NIV) says, "*What I am saying is that as long as the heir is a child, he is no different from a slave, although he owns the whole estate. He is subject to guardians and trustees until the time set by his father. God sent His Son, born of a woman, born under law, to redeem those under law, that we might receive the full rights of sons.*" Who is it that God considers sons? Those who have accepted Jesus Christ as Lord and Savior, those who obey His commands and promote His Kingdom, those who walk as sons, not as immature children. A child may be eligible but will not receive the blessing until s/he has demonstrated the maturity to receive it. Hebrews 5:11-14 (AMPL) addresses it this way:

> *Concerning this we have much to say which is hard to explain, since you have become dull in your [spiritual] hearing and sluggish, even slothful [in achieving spiritual insight]. For even though by this time you ought to be teaching others, you actually need someone to teach you over again the very first principles of God's Word. You have come to need milk, not solid food. For every one who continues to feed on milk is obviously inexperienced and unskilled in the doctrine of righteousness, [that is, of conformity to the Divine will in purpose, thought and action] for he is a mere infant—not able to talk yet! But solid food is for full-grown men, for those whose senses and mental faculties are trained by practice to discriminate and distinguish between what is morally good and noble and what is evil and contrary either to Divine or human law.*

At this point, I want us to fully understand what the Lord is giving us. In Isaiah 55:10-11 (MKJV), He says, *"For as the rain comes down, and the snow from the heavens, and does not return there, but waters the earth, and makes it bring out and bud, and give seed to the sower and bread to the eater; **so shall My Word be, which goes out of My mouth; it shall not return to Me void, but it shall accomplish what I please, and it shall certainly do what I sent it to do**."* In Jeremiah 1:12 (AMPL), the Lord says, *"For I am alert and active, watching over my word to perform it."* In Isaiah, we have a (covenant) promise from the Lord . . . His word will accomplish what it was sent to do. Then in Jeremiah, He emphasizes that not only will that word accomplish His desires but also that He will personally watch over that spoken word to ensure its effectiveness. In Jeremiah 32, He again confirms all of His promises by an oath sealed by His covenant. As if all of this was not enough, in the new dispensation of grace through the Lord Jesus Christ, we read in 1 Peter 3 that we have been called to inherit a blessing! So God Almighty speaks a blessing over us when we are obedient to fulfill His desires and then watches over that spoken word to ensure it accomplishes His intentions in the lives of His (obedient) children. What is our part in all of this? It is to unequivocally understand the heart of the Lord and to then step out in active and bold faith, so that our works will be an attestation of our faith, and the reality of our faith will be proven by our works.

The essence of partnership with the Lord lies in the foundational quintessence of (1) believing that He is, (2) believing that He exists, (3) believing that He is the *only* living God, (4) believing that He is the Creator of heaven and earth, (5) believing in His Son Jesus Christ—as Lord and Savior, (6) believing in the indwelling presence of the Holy Spirit as His gift to those who have accepted Jesus Christ as Lord and Savior, and (7) believing in His goodwill toward mankind and subsequent covenants He introduced.

The Lord God desires to bless and to prosper His children when they: firstly, walk in obedience to His commands in regard to partnership—first with Him and then with one another; secondly, when they comply with the conditions of His promises; and thirdly, when they walk fearlessly and in maturity in the fullness of His promised provision and blessing encapsulated within the (covenant) blessings. In Matthew 11:12, Jesus implies that we are to take the kingdom of heaven by force, meaning we are to stand with authority upon our rightful inheritance against the opposing forces from hell that are forever striving to circumvent the plans of God for His people and the world. It is only when we are operating through renewed and mature mindsets that we can stand in absolute unity and as a whole against the devil's attacks—and thwart His plans. As believers in and disciples of the Lord Jesus Christ, we have been given His absolute authority, so let's use it!

Partnership with each other as members of His redeemed family through the Lord Jesus Christ should be an attestation to the unsaved world of the Divine unity that exists amongst God's children. This very important factor should be so prevalent to the unsaved that it will act as a mark of distinction that would clearly draw the dividing line between those that are members of His household and those that are not.

In the Acts of the Apostles, chapters 4 and 5, we read how the oneness and the partnership amongst all who believed caused a great drawing factor that led to very rapid and dynamic growth and expansion of the body of believers. In Matthew 18:19 (AMPL), the Lord Jesus again gave us another example of the power and subsequent blessings contained within and for those who would partner first with Him and then with one another: *"Again I tell you, if two of you on earth agree (harmonize together, together make a symphony) about—anything and everything—whatever they shall ask, it will come to pass and be done for them by My Father in heaven."* Can you see the Lord's heart in this? His heart is to bless (prosper) those of His household far beyond their levels of expectation, because He wants them to have more, so they can give more, so they can have more, so they can give more, and . . . to subsequently use them to point all the unsaved in the direction of His Son, so all can inherit salvation. Satan is desperate to prevent that and has been far too successful in his efforts. Now is the time for God's people to realize that God's priorities are much bigger than our own little worlds, our own little denominational doctrines, and our own little comfort zones.

In these same chapters, we read how great miracles took place amongst those who were together: *"And the multitude of those who believed were of one heart and one soul. And not one said that any of the things which he possessed was his own. But they had all things common"* (Acts 4:32 MKJV). Acts 5:12 (MKJV) continues: *"And many miracles and wonders were done among the people by the hands of the apostles; and they were all with one accord in Solomon's Porch.*" Those miracles of healing and provision caused a drawing factor that brought great multitudes to accept the Lord Jesus Christ as Savior.

It is in the absolute unity amongst believers of the Lord Jesus Christ that the Holy Spirit will always manifest with subsequent signs, wonders, and miracles. This (simple) principle, when applied according to the original blueprint of the church as we find in the Acts of the Apostles, is the single most important factor for effective church growth.

We also need to understand, as explained before, that partnership with the Lord God will always have reproduction as a consequence: "*For your Maker is your husband; Jehovah of Hosts is His name; and your Redeemer is the Holy One of Israel; the God of the whole earth shall He be called*" (Isa. 54:6 MKJV). This scripture is just loaded with promises of reproduction for those whose husband is the Lord God Almighty. Firstly, He says He is our Husband. This speaks of a very intimate relationship—the kind that would normally exist between a husband and wife and which would normally produce children. Secondly, in confirmation of this, He says, "*The God of the whole earth shall He be called.*" This statement speaks of future tense and undoubtedly refers to the New Testament times when both the Jews and the Gentiles shall worship Him as God Almighty. Again we see the multiplication factor at work. The only way the Gentiles can learn about and accept Him as the only true God is by the continued testimony of individual believers who would, as a direct consequence of their partnership with the Lord, partner together, form a society of believers (church), and then continue to partner with others that would go out and proclaim the Word of the Lord and the Good News of the Gospel. Just as in marriage, a ministry should be reproducing spiritual children. Part of the blessing of covenant partnership is fruitfulness.

A simple corncob example will illustrate this better. We have seen, from Genesis to where we are today, that everything created by God was created with reproduction, continuity, and multiplication in mind. Let's look at God's standard of measure revealed in corn:
If you take one kernel and plant it, you will harvest on average two whole cobs of corn. Each cob will hold an average of about 500 kernels = seeds.

So in your first season of harvesting you will reap approximately 1,000 seeds. This is already a display of the Lord's standard of measure. But it will get even better . . .

Remember the parable of the talents. We are to work with what is given to us; we are not to eat our entire harvest, consuming it all on ourselves. If we plant all 1,000 seeds given to us, the equation will look like this: 1,000 seeds will produce 1,000 plants, each producing 2 cobs of corn, with each cob producing approximately 500 seeds.

So, 1,000 x 1,000 = 1,000,000 plants, which = 2,000,000 cobs, which = 1,000,000,000 seeds!

Obviously, we can continue with this process for eternity—providing we can find the land for it all. All of this started with just ONE seed! That is a perfect display of what the Lord has in mind when He speaks about multiplication, reproduction, and continuation when we work in partnership as He directs!

Let's use another example: In 2 Kings 4:1-7, we read the account of the widow who was about to loose her two sons as a result of outstanding debts. All she had left in her house was a small jar of oil. On Elisha's instructions, she borrows as many empty containers from her neighbors as she could and begins to pour the oil . . . and pour . . . and pour . . . and pour . . . She subsequently was able to miraculously fill all the containers from that one little jar, sell the oil, pay all her debts, and have plenty left over to provide for her and her sons. This incident was another illustration of the Lord's standard of measure. The flowing of the oil stopped only after she had no more empty jars to fill. There are several lessons we can learn from this, but the one I want us to focus on for the moment is this:

When we would partner with the Lord and use our faith to then also reach out and partner with a minister or ministry, we have an opportunity to keep pouring from what we have. If we are faithful and if we have enough "empty jars," the miracle of provision will continue to pour forth from heaven, meeting not only our needs but also providing more than what we need; so we can have much to give and give and give and give . . . The secret really is to keep pouring out. Ephesians 3:20-21 (AMPL) summarizes and promises this continuous provision in a beautiful way: *"Now to Him Who, by (in consequence of) the [action of His] power that is at work within us, is able to [carry out His purpose and] do superabundantly, far over and above all that we [dare] ask or think—infinitely beyond our highest prayers, desires, thoughts, hopes or dreams."*

In some circumstances, we find ourselves being the "neighbor" instead of the widow. What is our response when someone comes and asks us for something? I believe that not only did the Lord Jesus have a blessing in store for the widow but also for all those who would determine to partner with her, as a continuation of the ministry. Once the oil was sold and the jars returned to their rightful owners, culturally they would have been returned with a blessing. This is the principle of "give, and it will be given to you" in action.

Unfortunately, this is not the case so many times today. When asked for something, we tend to hold back, to not want to give, to hoard what we have. Why is that, if we truly understand "give, and it will be given"? Because, unfortunately, most people do not understand partnership, and so when they are blessed, they take the blessing without turning around and giving that blessing back again. It is difficult when you give and give and no one gives in return, and this leads to the mentality of protecting oneself first at all costs.

In the example of the widow, what if one of the widow's neighbors had chosen not to loan her a jar? Not only would the widow's blessing been limited but the neighbor's as well. In other words, the neighbor's act of righteousness, of partnering together with a ministry to help in a time of need, ended up being credited to their account. They not only got back what they gave out (their jar) but also more. In essence, they were able to become partakers of the widow's—the ministry's—harvest.

This very same principle applies when we partner with those who are doing the work the Lord directs. We can rest assured that when we partner with God's appointed and anointed ministries, God will count the salvation and deliverance of every individual who comes to that saving knowledge of the Lord Jesus as a result of such partnership(s), to the account of every believer who supports the efforts of the church and itinerant ministers. Too many times Christians are too quick to say, "God bless you, my brother," and forget about the essence of true giving and sharing. In James 2:15-17

(BBE), the Bible teaches us: *"If a brother or a sister is without clothing and in need of the day's food, And one of you says to them, Go in peace, be warm and full of food; but you do not give them the things of which their bodies have need, what profit is there in this? Even so faith without works is dead."* The Message translation on verse 17 says, *"Isn't it obvious that God-talk without God-acts is outrageous nonsense?"*

As was the case with the Apostles, God does not appoint every one of His ministers to pastor a church. There are five different offices for His appointed ministers, i.e., Apostle, Prophet, Pastor, Teacher, and Evangelist. Each office has its own peculiar anointing and calling. It is of vital importance for every believer to be exposed to the teachings of each of these offices and not only that, but also to partner with some of these ministries beyond and through their churches. If God has called a person to an itinerant ministry, God will hold the church—corporately and individually—responsible for partnering with, taking care of, and providing for the needs of that person. Once again, the leading of and obedience to the Holy Spirit as to whom we should partner with is of crucial importance. Always remember, to partner with a Holy Spirit-established ministry is to partner with the Lord Himself.

The Lord emphasizes this exact principle in 3 John 1:5-8 (NLT):

> *Dear friend, **you are being faithful to God** when you care for the traveling teachers who pass through, even though they are strangers to you. They have told the church here of your loving friendship. **Please continue providing for such teachers in a manner that pleases God.** For they are traveling for the Lord, and they accept nothing from people who are not believers. So we ourselves should support them so that we can be their partners as they teach the truth."* The Amplified translation puts verse 8 this way: *"So we ourselves ought to support such people—**to welcome and provide for them**—in order that we may be fellow workers in the Truth (the whole Gospel) and co-operate with its teachers.*

When members of a congregation will truly partner with one another in the same way as those early believers did, and when they will then reach out to also partner with others of God's household called by Him and sent to proclaim His message outside of the walls of the church, we have the promise from the Lord Jesus that God Almighty *will* answer and *will* provide our needs and bless us according to His standard of measure, which is a "*good measure, pressed down, shaken together, and running over.*"

What is God's ultimate goal for this earth? Second Peter 3:9 (GW) says, "*The Lord isn't slow to do what He promised, as some people think. Rather, He is patient for your sake. He doesn't want to destroy anyone* **but wants all people to have an opportunity to turn to Him and change the way they think and act.**" John 3:17 (MKJV) says, "*For God did not send His Son into the world to condemn the world,* **but so that the world might be saved through Him.**" The Lord God accomplished this desire, this goal of His, through the Lord Jesus Christ: "*For it pleased the Father that in Him all fullness should dwell. And through Him having made peace through the blood of His cross, it pleased the Father to reconcile all things to Himself through Him, whether the things on earth or the things in Heaven*" (Col. 1:19-20 MKJV). It is the moral and spiritual responsibility of every Christian in this world today to work in partnership with the Lord and in a combined partnership with each other to spread this wonderful gospel to every living soul.

The truth in Colossians 1:9-12 (AMPL) emphasizes exactly this fundamental principle:

> *For this reason we also, from the day we heard of it, have not ceased to pray and make [special] request for you, [asking] that you might be filled with the full (deep and clear) knowledge of His will in all spiritual wisdom [that is, in comprehensive insight into the ways and purposes of God] and in understanding and discernment of spiritual things;* **That you may live (walk and conduct yourselves) in a manner worthy of the Lord, fully pleasing to Him and desiring to please Him in all things, bearing fruit in every good work,** *and steadily growing and increasing in (and by) the knowledge of God—with fuller, deeper and clearer insight, acquaintance and recognition. We pray that you be invigorated and strengthened with all power, according to the might of His glory [to exercise] every kind of endurance*

and patience (perseverance and forebearance) with Joy. Giving thanks to the Father, Who has qualified and fit to share the portion which is the inheritance of the saints (God's holy people) in the light.

The Message translation quotes verse 10 this way:

We pray that you'll live well for the Master, making Him proud of you as you work hard in His orchard. As you learn more and more how God works, you will learn how to do your work.

Chapter 4

WORKS OF FAITH . . . IN FAITH

In order to walk in the light of the marvelous truth contained within Colossians 1:9-12, we must ask ourselves the following questions: Is it possible to partner with the Lord without believing in Him, and conversely, can we believe in Him without partnering with Him? To partner with the Lord is to display His virtues to the world. Isaiah 58:7 sets forth some of these virtues: sharing food with the hungry, providing shelter for the wanderer, clothing the naked, etc. Jesus, speaking in Matthew 25:34-40 (MKJV), continues His teachings with these same standards:

> *Then the King shall say to those on His right hand, Come, blessed of My Father, inherit the kingdom prepared for you from the foundation of the world. For I was hungry, and you gave me food; I was thirsty, and you gave Me drink; I was a stranger, and you took Me in; I was naked, and you clothed Me; I was sick, and you visited Me; I was in prison, and you came to Me. Then the righteous shall answer Him, saying, Lord, when did we see You hungry, and fed You? Or thirsty, and gave You drink? When did we see You a stranger, and took You in? Or naked, and*

clothed You? Or when did we see You sick, or in prison, and came to You? And the King shall answer and say to them, Truly I say to you, Inasmuch as you did it to one of the least of these My brothers, you have done it to Me.

There are many philanthropists who display these Kingdom virtues without confessing Jesus as Savior and Lord. They do many wonderful works and frequently bring great relief in humanitarian aid. Unfortunately, they are not in the position of an heir to receive the ultimate blessing and inheritance of eternal life themselves because of their lack of covenant relationship with God through Jesus Christ. We are to convey the message of salvation to these people, so they can understand that their good deeds will not and cannot buy their eternal destiny with God. The Bible—the Word of God—is very clear and very specific: "*Jesus said to him, I am the Way, the Truth, and the Life; no one comes to the Father but by Me*" (John 14:6 MKJV). Many of these people believe that their good deeds will "earn them points" with God one day when they have to face Him. Sadly, this is not the case because once again the Word of God is very specific: "*For by grace you are saved through faith, and that not of yourselves, it is the gift of God, not of works, lest anyone should boast*" (Eph. 2:8-9 MKJV).

In Isaiah 64:6 (AMPL), the prophet laments over the hopelessness of humanity in the presence of God without a mediator—a savior. He specifically addresses the futility of any effort to impress or sway the influence of God through acts of giving, or acts of "righteousness": "*For we have all become as one who is unclean (ceremonially, as a leper), and all our righteousness—our best deeds of rightness and justice—are as filthy rags, or a polluted garment. We all fade as a leaf, and our iniquities, like the wind, take us away (far from God's favor, hurrying us to destruction).*" The *Douay Rheims Bible Translation* translates the "filthy rags" as "the rag of a menstruous woman." This is the correct translation and is derived from the original Aramaic word *ed*, pronounced "ayd." This word was used to indicate the absolute repugnance of "deeds of righteousness" when used in an effort to sway the mind of God. The great tragedy is that there are many from God's own household who adhere to this abhorrent practice without understanding the insult and rejection it carries to God the Father and Christ the Redeemer.

The other unfortunate truth is that many of these philanthropists are also doing these "good deeds" for other benefits, such as tax deductions and to receive recognition from society in order to promote themselves and their own programs or businesses. Yet again we have another clear directive from the Lord Jesus in this regard: "*Therefore when you do your merciful deeds, do not sound a trumpet before you, as the hypocrites do in the synagogues and in the streets, so that they may have glory from men. Truly I say to you, they have their reward*" (Matt. 6:2 MKJV). The Lord is simply saying that people who use acts (of benevolence) to impress others (society) can never claim their reward from God . . . they have already received their due reward from those they sought to impress for personal gain, and they have not been accepted as His partners because they are not working in His vineyard but their own. Remember, partnership is an agreement between two or more parties to work together toward a common goal.

We should not be so arrogant as to think that our partnering with God has suddenly "empowered" Him. As much as we should willingly agree to partner with Him, so much so will it be for our benefit to understand that He Himself must also agree to accept us as His partners, as His co-workers. The qualifying criterion for God to accept us is when we accept Jesus Christ as Lord and Savior. As always, let's go to the Word of God to verify this statement: "*But when the kindness and love of God our Savior toward man appeared, not by works of righteousness which we have done, but according to His mercy He saved us, through the washing of regeneration and renewal of the Holy Spirit, whom **He poured out on us abundantly through Jesus Christ our Savior, that being justified by His grace, we should become heirs according to the hope of eternal life**" (Titus 3:4-7 MKJV). The Amplified Bible translates verse 7 as follows: "(*And He did it in order) that we might be justified by His grace—by His favor, wholly undeserved, that is, **that we might be acknowledged and counted as conformed to the Divine will in purpose, thought and action;** and that we might become heirs of eternal life according to our hope.*"

It is then when we accept God's gift of eternal life through Jesus Christ with a willing, repenting, and humble heart that we will be accepted as worthy to be called His partners, that we will be made acceptable through Jesus and will be qualified and called upon to act as ambassadors representing His Kingdom. **This should always be a yardstick to all**

who enter into partnership with the Lord. All of our efforts toward promoting His business should always, always come from a pure heart motivation with one goal only: to enable His wonderful Gospel and His Kingdom values to be proclaimed and taught to all peoples on the earth. The Lord Jesus Christ is God's gift to all mankind—to whosoever shall believe. To bypass Him is to reject God's qualifying gift and, as we've seen above in John 14:6 and now in Acts 4:12, is rejecting the only way to the Father. *"And there is salvation in no other One; for there is no other name under Heaven given among men by which we must be saved"* (Acts 4:12 MKJV).

In Hebrews 6:10 (MKJV), we find the determining key for doing benevolent acts with the right heart motivation: *"For God is not unrighteous to forget your work and labor of love **which you have shown toward His name**, in that you have ministered to the saints, and do minister."* I want to share with you the hidden nugget revealed in this scripture. It says, *"Your work and labor of love which you have shown **toward His name**."* The English word *name* or *His name* is derived from the Greek word *onoma*, which is used in the context of authority and character. So to read this scripture in context, we should read it like this: *"For God is not unrighteous to forget your work and labor of love which you have shown toward* [His authority, His character, and His name] *in that you have ministered to the saints, and do minister."* So simply put, our acts of benevolence should always be done honoring HIM and pointing to HIM as the ultimate provider and source for the meeting of every need.

Even though the "saints"—God's people—are the benefactors of such giving, our partnership with the Lord should be the only catalyst in our motivation. Understand this fundamental principle: Unless God provides we will have nothing to give. The very fact that we are in a position to give should always be for His glory as we humbly acknowledge Him as the Great Provider (El Shaddai), the initiator in the process of giving. I will deal with this in more detail in a subsequent chapter.

Just as there are those who display Kingdom virtues without entering into the Kingdom itself by faith in Jesus Christ, so there are those who display the reciprocal. There are many who have accepted Jesus Christ as Savior and Lord, confessing Him with their mouths, yet are not partnering with Him actively to advance His Kingdom not only in their own lives but also in the lives of those they come into contact with. Jesus says, in Matthew 15:8 (NIV): *"These people honor Me with their lips, but their hearts are far from Me."* Instead of passionately demonstrating their faith in the Lord, they become or never move out of passivity and lethargy and therefore never, or at the best only occasionally, partner with Him and His ministry. The result is the same: they forever remain a "child," never stepping into a position to receive the full blessing and inheritance of the saints that God intends for them to receive as mature sons and daughters. Just as presenting our acts to God as acts of self-righteousness is abhorrent to Him, so much so is our lack of commitment to live out our faith and pledge to Him. Revelation 3:15-16 (AMPL) says, *"I know your [record of] works and what you are doing; you are neither cold nor hot. Would that you were cold or hot! So, because you are lukewarm, and neither cold nor hot, I will spew you out of my mouth!"*

We cannot separate our faith in Jesus Christ from our works. There are several things clear from this passage. First is that God detests someone being lukewarm to the point that He would rather you are against Him than to be lukewarm: *"Would that you were cold or hot!"* This is a very serious, strong stance from the Lord. Second is the definition of the word for *works* used in this passage. It means "deed, labor, or work," but it also means "toil, as in an occupation." This indicates not just once off or occasional acts of works for His Kingdom but a committed lifestyle of such. Third is the word used for *spew*, which is *emeo,* meaning, "to vomit." From a physical standpoint, you are stimulated to vomit when you overeat, eat something spoiled, eat something poisonous; experience intense emotion; have infections within the body; or have a reaction to certain smells or odors. We can therefore apply this and say that when we are lukewarm, God has such a negative intense emotional reaction (in the form of detesting) to our being lukewarm that it is like He ate something spoiled, rotten, or poisonous to Himself.

James 2:14-26, in The Message translation, gives us a Divine perspective of our individual responsibility as well as provides us with a yardstick to measure our faith:

> *Dear friends, do you think you'll get anywhere in this if you learn all the right words but never do anything? Does merely talking about faith indicate that a person really has*

it? For instance, you come upon an old friend dressed in rags and half-starved and say, 'Good morning, friend! Be clothed in Christ! Be filled with the Holy Spirit!' and walk off without providing so much as a coat or a cup of soup—where does that get you? Isn't it obvious that God-talk without God-acts is outrageous nonsense? I can already hear one of you agreeing by saying, 'Sounds good. You take care of the faith department, I'll handle the works department.' Not so fast. You can no more show me your works apart from your faith than I can show you my faith apart from my works. Faith and works, works and faith, fit together hand in glove. Do I hear you professing to believe in the one and only God, but then observe you complacently sitting back as if you had done something wonderful? That's just great. Demons do that, but what good does it do them? Use your heads! Do you suppose for a minute that you can cut faith and works in two and not end up with a corpse on your hands? Wasn't our ancestor Abraham 'made right with God by works' when he placed his son Isaac on the sacrificial altar? Isn't it obvious that faith and works are yoked partners, that faith expresses itself in works? That the works are 'works of faith'? The full meaning of 'believe' in the Scripture sentence, 'Abraham believed God and was set right with God,' includes his action. It's that mesh of believing and acting that got Abraham named 'God's friend.' Is it not evident that a person is made right with God not by a barren faith but by faith fruitful in works? The same with Rahab, the Jericho harlot. Wasn't her action in hiding God's spies and helping them escape—that seamless unity of believing and doing—what counted with God? The very moment you separate body and spirit, you end up with a corpse. Separate faith and works and you get the same thing: a corpse.

The *Matthew Henry's Concise Commentary* gives us the following insights:

This place of Scripture plainly shows that an opinion, or assent to the gospel, without works, is not faith. There is no way to show we really believe in Christ, but by being diligent in good works, from gospel motives, and for gospel purposes. Men may boast to others, and be conceited of that which they really have not. There is not only to be assent in faith, but consent; not only an assent to the truth of the word, but a consent to take Christ. **True believing is not an act of the understanding only, but a work of the whole heart.** That a justifying faith cannot be without works, is shown from two examples, Abraham and Rahab. Abraham believed God, and it was reckoned unto him for righteousness. Faith, producing such works, advanced him to peculiar favours. We see then, James 2:24, how that by works a man is justified, not by a bare opinion or profession, or believing without obeying; **but by having such faith as produces good works.** And to have to deny his own reason, affections, and interests, is an action fit to try a believer. Observe here, the wonderful power of faith in changing sinners. Let us then take heed, for the best works, without faith, are dead; they want root and principle. By faith, any thing we do is really good as done in obedience to God, and aiming at his acceptance: the root is as though it were dead, when there is no fruit. **Faith is the root, good works are the fruits; and we must see to it that we have both.** This is the grace of God wherein we stand, and we should stand to it. **There is no middle state. Every one must either live as God's friend, or God's enemy. Living to God, as it is the consequence of faith, which justifies and will save, obliges us to do nothing against him, but every thing for him and to him.**

The lukewarm state of being, as mentioned by the Lord in Revelation 3, has unfortunately permeated many Christian denominations and societies, because the full essence and benefits of partnership is not fully understood and has subsequently become a passive concept. In pastors' meetings, the common denominator of complaints is the lack of commitment amongst the greater majority of congregants in their churches. In most churches the actual percentage (compared to the whole) of God's children that are active participants is dismally low, and we need to ask ourselves why. This unfortunate truth is a very disappointing reality among those who call themselves Christians, who confess Jesus Christ as Lord and Savior but who will do absolutely nothing or, at best, as little as possible to promote His Gospel and His word to be preached to the world outside of their own little worlds.

Passivity in the Kingdom of God is activity in satan's kingdom, and every person who calls him/herself a Christian will do well to realize this dangerous zone. The real tragedy of such passivity is the absolute absence of any form of real heartfelt love toward the Lord. The greatest commandment we as Christians have received from our God and our Savior is this: *"And Jesus answered him, 'The first of all the commandments is, "Hear, O Israel, the Lord our God is one Lord; and you shall love the **Lord your God with all your heart, and with all your soul, and with all your mind, and with all your strength**." This is the first commandment. And the second is like this: **You shall love your neighbor as yourself.** There is no other commandment greater than these'"* (Mark 12:29-31 MKJV). The Amplified translation augments the absolute dynamics of these great commandments:

> *Jesus answered, The first and principal one of all commandments is, Hear, O Israel: The Lord our God is one Lord; **And you shall love the Lord your God out of and with your whole heart, and out of and with all your soul (your life) and out of and with all your mind—(that is) with your faculty of thought and your moral understanding—and out of and with all your strength.** This is the first and principal commandment. The second **is like it and is this; You shall love your neighbor as yourself.** There is no other commandment greater than these.*

The Lord Jesus is saying that our love for the Lord our God, if it is really a true heartfelt love, should compel us to love our neighbor—even as we love ourselves. In other words, that same LOVE we have for the Lord should be the same LOVE we have for our neighbor. He makes no distinction of emotion but categorically declares, "***The second is like it and is this***." The word *love* in these scriptures is derived from the Greek word *agapao*, which is used to indicate absolute love—not a mere fondness but a love that is compelling in its essence—a love that is unconditional. True love, agape love, is always demonstrated by what we do, not by what we say.

In Mark 12:42-44, we find what is to me one of the most beautiful love stories hidden in the pages of the Bible. It is the recording of the poor widow who came to the treasury (offering box) to present an offering to the Lord. She put in the last money she had—the equivalent of two cents. This widow loved the Lord so much that she was prepared to prove her love for Him with everything that represents her livelihood—in absolute trust and confidence and in complete obedience to His word. She believed and loved the Lord with the same unconditional love as she would her husband. In her case, it was so noteworthy that the Lord Jesus called His disciples' attention to it and also chose to have it recorded in His book of remembrance as an example of true love, commitment, and partnership. She would most definitely have received a very great eternal reward for that small little offering—an offering that was noted by God Almighty as if it was the greatest gift He's ever received. In Jeremiah 17:10 (NLT), the Lord says, "*But I, the LORD, search all hearts and examine secret motives. I give all people their due rewards, according to what their actions deserve.*"

In order to emphasize this, the Lord Jesus then told His disciples, "*If you love me, **show it by doing what I've told you**"* (John 14:15 MSG). Here we find the emphasis on the verb *doing*, which calls for action—in continuous future tense. How can we say we love our neighbor—who is everybody—but then withhold support from those who are called to bring the good news of Salvation to those neighbors who have not yet heard it and have not been given the opportunity to meet their Savior, Jesus Christ? How can we, as individual and corporate believers, face our God one day in the hope of receiving His warm welcome when we hear the cries of those neighbors that have gone to hell because we have not done our part in giving them an opportunity to hear the Gospel? That is hypocrisy in its worst form. If you are one of those who have not been active in your partnership with the Lord, one of those who have not done your full share to work in His vineyard, then go to Him in repentance and make amends. Seek Him now for guidance as to whom **He** wants you to partner with. Leave no stone untouched and follow through!

Everything that God creates is good, because God is only good. Satan is the reciprocal to this. In him there is no good at all; there is only darkness and evil. There is nothing that God has created that satan won't twist, contort, and rape for his own purpose, which is to get everyone to rebel against God as he did. He is like a Trojan horse, working from the inside out to destroy our lives, our relationship with others and most importantly with God and, subsequently, our productivity for God's Kingdom. He may not be able to keep you from salvation in the Lord Jesus Christ, but he certainly can inactivate you, incapacitate you, and make you unproductive. Jesus, speaking in Mathew 12:30 and again in Luke 11:23 (MKJV), says, *"The one who is not with Me is against Me, and the one who does not gather with me, scatters."* The Message translation puts it this way: ***"This is war, and there is no neutral ground. If you're not on My side, you're the enemy. If you're not helping, you're making things worse."*** The message of these verses could not be clearer: you are either productive for God's kingdom or you are productive for satan's kingdom—period. Being unproductive—being neutral, passive, and lukewarm—by default sets us against God, because we are not advancing His cause and we are not gathering for His Kingdom, which is exactly what satan wants.

The concepts of partnership involve and saturate every aspect of our society: from business, friendship, churches, political parties and candidates, our favorite sports teams, to marriage. The question is . . . how far have we strayed from God's original intent and design of partnership within these unions? A fundamental aspect of partnership is that it will require sacrifice on each person's part; yet how willing are we to do this? Our example and foundation in any partnership should be God the Father and God the Son. *"For God so loved the world that He gave His only begotten Son"* (John 3:16 MKJV). God was willing to sacrifice something very precious to Himself for the bigger picture: His Son. *"No one has greater love than this, that a man lay down his life for his friends"* (John 15:13 MKJV). Jesus was willing to sacrifice something very precious for the benefit of all mankind: His life!

True partnership is not a self-centered association, which unfortunately is what is too commonly found. Partnership requires giving on both sides—not just taking. There are many who will say they do contribute to those they are in partnership with—financially. They "give" to their church and to the "big" ministries. No doubt, this giving is very important; but financial giving is only a small portion of what giving (tithes and offerings) and, subsequently, partnership is all about. In the Old Testament, it was God who laid down the requirements of bringing tithes and offerings to the temple, and it wasn't just money that was brought originally; there were also grains, birds, and animals. The Israelites brought, first and foremost, as an act of worship unto the Lord God and to honor Him as the ultimate giver and provider. Yet in doing so, they were activating a fundamental concept of God's Kingdom. They, in their giving, by default in that action, became an extension of God's hand of provision, blessing, and partnership to and for the priests and their families. **Through obedience to God's ordinance of giving, they became a continuation of His Divine nature.** God takes a very personal interest in how congregations are treating their Pastors and visiting Ministers.

In Nehemiah, chapter 13, we read how the temple of the Lord was abandoned because the people failed to bring their tithes and offerings. The Levites and the singers left the temple to find employment elsewhere, and as a result, the temple failed in its purpose because it received nothing, had nothing, and consequently gave nothing. It gave no spiritual foundation to the nation; on the contrary, it allowed the nation to regress to spiritual prostitution. Because of this, it failed in its Divine intent and purpose, and therefore, because of this failure, it also received nothing and consequently it could give nothing. In verse 11, Nehemiah confronted the rulers with a question that still resounds today: "Why is the house of God forsaken?"

This was a classical example of God's people not having a true relationship with their God and with "rulers" who could not maintain and counsel the nation to stay true to their God. When the house of God is forsaken, when the house of God is left to the "rulers," then the nation will perish. When we "de-partner" with God, we place ourselves on a course of collision with our Almighty Creator because we sever ourselves from the Ultimate Provider and, by default, side with the ultimate destroyer—satan.

There is, never has been, nor will there ever be a recession in heaven, yet believers and churches are quick to declare this reality as an absolute in their own finances. God is Almighty; God has created the entire universe from nothing, and God is certainly not limited in His ability to provide for His church. He did not need Wall Street to determine His profitability, nor did He need any human currency to create the universe. God is not and never has been neither influenced nor dependent upon any form of worldly currency. There is no problem with heaven's finances—there is no recession in heaven. If God's people, who would like to call themselves by His name, *Christ*-ians, would truly partner with God and with each other in terms of the original Divine intent, the church—His body of believers—would set the standard for the world and will not hear the question: "Why is the house of God forsaken?"

The foundational principles of partnership amongst God's people should once again be seen as an opportunity to direct unbelievers to the Lord during financially stressed times. Unfortunately, many believers and, subsequently, churches have chosen to side with the world and will boldly proclaim and lament on the reduced income as a result of the "recession," instead of proclaiming the absolute truth of the Word of God, which says, *"But my God shall supply all your needs according to His riches in glory by Christ Jesus"* (Phil. 4:19 MKJV). This promise from the Lord is once again conditional: our riches will be supplied—ACCORDING TO His riches and glory through Christ Jesus. When the church fails in its mission, as we've seen in Nehemiah 13, then that failure will determine the same provision because of the yardstick "according to."

Scripture is clear, the temple—the church—failed in its mission because the people (Believers . . . ?) stopped giving. The people would have only stopped giving because they never had a true worshipful relationship and partnership with their God and, consequently, never entered into partnership with Him or one another to promote His business more than their own. If a church would stop inviting itinerant ministers because the church's income has dropped, then that church is opposing the will of God, is denying the different ministerial offices God has set in place, and is simply continuing with the same mindset as that of the people that Nehemiah found in Jerusalem, who caused the Levites and singers to leave the church. *"But if anyone does not provide for his own, and especially his family, he has denied the faith and is worse than an infidel"* (1Tim. 5:8 MKJV). In Galatians 6:10 (MKJV), the Word of God teaches us: *"So then as we have time, let us work good toward all, **especially*** *toward those of the household of faith*." The household of faith is God's household where we are all to labor in union and partnership—firstly, as His partners, His ambassadors, and, secondly, in partnership with one another toward our common goal.

Partnership is an agreement between two or more persons to collaborate, to team up, to join and work together toward a common purpose in a joint venture, and to unify and combine all abilities and resources in order to accomplish that purpose. **Partnership is also companionship, friendship and, camaraderie, with the intent of surrounding one another for the mutual benefit of aiding and protecting one another**.

Remember what Jesus said: "*For whoever shall give you a cup of water to drink in My name, because you belong to Christ, truly I say to you, He shall not lose his reward*" (Mark 9:41 MKJV).

Giving, in its broadest context, is a law of relationship (and partnership). This concept of Divine partnership, of bringing not only your finances but also other material possessions and your God-given talents toward a common purpose, is illustrated so beautifully in Exodus, chapters 35 and 36, in the building of the tabernacle:

> *Moses spoke to all the congregation of the children of Israel, saying, 'This is the thing which Yahweh commanded, saying, Take from among you an offering to Yahweh. Whoever is of a willing heart, let him bring it, Yahweh's offering: gold, silver, brass, blue, purple, scarlet, fine linen, goats' hair, rams' skins dyed red, sea cow hides, acacia wood, oil for the light, spices for the anointing oil and for the sweet incense, onyx stones, and stones to be set for the ephod and for the breastplate. Let every wise-hearted man among you come, and make all that Yahweh has commanded.' They came, everyone whose heart stirred him up, and everyone whom his spirit made willing, and brought Yahweh's offering, for the work of the tent of meeting, and for all of its service, and for the holy garments. They came, both men and women, as many as were willing-hearted, and brought brooches, ear-rings,*

signet-rings, and armlets, all jewels of gold; even every man who offered an offering of gold to Yahweh. Everyone, with whom was found blue, purple, scarlet, fine linen, goats' hair, rams' skins dyed red, and sea cow hides, brought them. Everyone who did offer an offering of silver and brass brought Yahweh's offering; and everyone, with whom was found acacia wood for any work of the service, brought it. All the women who were wise-hearted spun with their hands, and brought that which they had spun, the blue, the purple, the scarlet, and the fine linen. All the women whose heart stirred them up in wisdom spun the goats' hair. The rulers brought the onyx stones, and the stones to be set, for the ephod and for the breastplate; and the spice, and the oil for the light, for the anointing oil, and for the sweet incense. The children of Israel brought a freewill offering to Yahweh; every man and woman, whose heart made them willing to bring for all the work, which Yahweh had commanded to be made by Moses. Moses said to the children of Israel, 'Behold, Yahweh has called by name Bezalel the son of Uri, the son of Hur, of the tribe of Judah. He has filled him with the Spirit of God, in wisdom, in understanding, in knowledge, and in all manner of workmanship; and to make skillful works, to work in gold, in silver, in brass, in cutting of stones for setting, and in carving of wood, to work in all kinds of skillful workmanship. He has put in his heart that he may teach, both he, and Oholiab, the son of Ahisamach, of the tribe of Dan. He has filled them with wisdom of heart, to work all manner of workmanship, of the engraver, of the skillful workman, and of the embroiderer, in blue, in purple, in scarlet, and in fine linen, and of the weaver, even of those who do any workmanship, and of those who make skillful works.' Moses called Bezalel and Oholiab, and every wise-hearted man, in whose heart Yahweh had put wisdom, even everyone whose heart stirred him up to come to the work to do it: and they received from Moses all the offering which the children of Israel had brought for the work of the service of the sanctuary, with which to make it.

The people brought their gold and their silver. They brought their "brooches, ear-rings, signet-rings, and armlets, all jewels of gold." What a symbolic sacrifice; these were "worldly" items, valuable and costly things men and women utilized to adorn themselves with that they were willingly giving up for the work of the Lord. But in addition to this, they brought so much more. What would have happened if they brought all these things, laid them at the feet of Moses, and then walked away? Who would have built the tabernacle? Only Bezalel and Oholiab? Instead, they also brought whatever ability and skill they had and donated it in partnership for the building of the temple: gold, silver, and brass workers; jewelers to set stones; wood carvers and engravers; spinners of cloth, embroiderers, and weavers; and teachers. So many people so unselfishly brought and contributed that, in the end, the people had to be restrained from bringing any more.

God did not design partnership to be a passive one-sided relationship but an active participation of all parties involved. To be passive means "not acting, but acted upon." This denotes a one-sided relationship: one person being the giver and one person being the recipient, one person sacrificing, with the other person reaping the benefits. God, even in the gift of salvation, did not mean it to be a passive process. The gift of salvation is a free gift in that we cannot purchase or earn our own salvation. It is through belief in Jesus Christ and His sanctifying work at Calvary that we are saved; so in that regard, it is "free." However, the gift of salvation also includes accepting Jesus Christ as LORD, which means subjecting our wants, our desires, and ourselves to Him and His will and working as a fellow worker together with Him for advancing His Kingdom.

It seems to me that this fundamental aspect of accepting, inviting, and submitting to His Lordship is quite often not emphasized and explained at the time of conversion and subsequently produces superficial commitments from new believers. New believers must be informed of the cost of discipleship at the time of conversion prior to being led in the prayer of salvation, so that the individual can make a quality decision. At the very least, it should be taught as a foundational principle to all new believers. One of the problems we have in the church and in ministries is that we have converts trying to make disciples.

Sharing the Gospel has sadly often become only a means of increasing numbers, revenue, and status, and not making true disciples of the Lord Jesus Christ. The Bible prophesies of the "great falling away" before the return of our Savior, and I believe the church (at large) is directly responsible for creating an entire culture of converts who do not understand that there is a cost to accepting Jesus as Lord, and sadly, they would be the first ones who would fall away when the testing of their faith comes.

Those (false) shepherds will also be held accountable for this. Evangelists and Pastors who are only interested in producing numbers as a means of procuring more money, status, and recognition will have a rude awakening waiting for them when they have to face Him on their day of reckoning. They compel believers to partner with them and their ministries, teaching them to "give in order to get," or "fake it till you make it." Such "giving" and "partnership" is completely devoid of love, worship, and honor for the Lord and is simply a spirit of pride, covetousness, selfishness, and lust for material gain. Conversely, those sheep who are choosing to base their beliefs on what such charismatic teachers are saying, instead of on the Word of God, will also have to give an account. From Genesis to Revelation, the pages of the Bible are filled with teachings and warnings against such fallacies and heathenistic beliefs. From God's perspective, we do not gain status when we are partnering with or are in association with some "well-known" minister or ministry—as if that will somehow elevate us above the rest.

Several years ago, a "well-known" minister friend of mine shared some profound "revelation" he had. He said to me, "Based on the law of sowing and reaping, if you sow into the poor, you'll reap poorly." I was shocked—to say the least! His "revelation" is a contradiction to everything the Lord Jesus is teaching us. Jesus Himself never went to the "leaders" to be known as being in association with them so He can promote His ministry, or to gain status, credibility, revenue, or acceptance amongst the people. No! He went to the unknown, the beggars, the lepers, the tax collectors, the outcasts of society, because it was to them that God chose to reveal Himself.

The essence of our partnership with the Lord Jesus was beautifully captured by Himself when He said:

When the Son of Man comes in His glory, and all the angels with Him, He will sit on His throne in heavenly glory. All the nations will be gathered before Him, and He will separate the people one from another as a shepherd separates the sheep from the goats. He will put the sheep on His right and the goats on His left. Then the King will say to those on His right, 'Come, you who are blessed by My Father; take your inheritance, the kingdom prepared for you since the creation of the world. For I was hungry and you gave Me something to eat, I was thirsty and you gave Me something to drink, I was a stranger and you invited Me in, I needed clothes and you clothed Me, I was sick and you looked after Me, I was in prison and you came to visit Me.' Then the righteous will answer Him, 'Lord, when did we see You hungry and feed You, or thirsty and give You something to drink? When did we see You a stranger and invite You in, or needing clothes and clothe You? When did we see You sick or in prison and go to visit You?' The King will reply, 'I tell you the truth, whatever you did for one of the least of these brothers of mine, you did for Me.' (Matt. 25:31-4 NIV)

When we partner with the Lord as our primary focus, He will direct us to sometimes partner with "unlikely" people, but we need to trust Him and be obedient to His direction and not be driven or motivated by selfish desires. My answer to this "informed" minister was that his "revelation" gives me good reason to never sow into his ministry, because he was obviously one of the poor—poor in spirit!

Understand this: The price the Lord Jesus paid for our salvation was a very, very costly price, and therefore, our full self-sacrificial commitment to and partnership with **Him** should reflect the value we add to what He accomplished on our behalf at Calvary. If our commitment is shallow, then it was "easy come" and it will be "easy go." Everything in God's Kingdom is of value, and anything of value should cost you—to add value. Salvation is not a matter of easy come, easy go. It is through salvation in Jesus Christ that we have a righteous relationship with God. There is nothing in this world that is of more value than this, and we should foster and pursue that relationship as the most prized possession we have on this earth—and for eternity.

The Message Bible, translated for "modern-day" language, sometimes gives us a very accurate translation able to encompass the heart and motive of the speaker. In this regard, I could find no better example to emphasize exactly how important this truth of sharing the cost of discipleship and partnership is in the understanding of a new believer. Matthew 7:12-16 and 21-27 says,

> *Here is a simple, rule-of-thumb guide for behavior: Ask yourself what you want people to do for you, then grab the initiative and do it for them. Add up God's Law and Prophets and this is what you get.* **Don't look for shortcuts to God. The market is flooded with surefire, easygoing formulas for a successful life that can be practiced in your spare time. Don't fall for that stuff, even though crowds of people do. The way to life—to God!—is vigorous and requires total attention.** *Be wary of false preachers who smile a lot, dripping with practiced sincerity. Chances are they are out to rip you off some way or other.* **Don't be impressed with charisma; look for character. Who preachers are is the main thing, not what they say. A genuine leader will never exploit your emotions or your pocketbook.** *These diseased trees with their bad apples are going to be chopped down and burned. Knowing the correct password—saying 'Master, Master,' for instance—isn't going to get you anywhere with me.* **What is required is serious obedience—doing what my Father wills.** *I can see it now—at the Final Judgment thousands strutting up to me and saying, 'Master, we preached the Message, we bashed the demons, our God-sponsored projects had everyone talking.' And do you know what I am going to say? 'You missed the boat. All you did was use me to make yourselves important. You don't impress me one bit. You're out of here.'* **These words I speak to you are not incidental additions to your life, homeowner improvements to your standard of living. They are foundational words, words to build**

a life on. If you work these words into your life, you are like a smart carpenter who built his house on solid rock. Rain poured down, the river flooded, a tornado hit—but nothing moved that house. It was fixed to the rock. But if *you just use my words in Bible studies and don't work them into your life, you are like a stupid carpenter who built his house on the sandy beach. When a storm rolled in and the waves came up, it collapsed like a house of cards.*

I have seen through many years of ministry just how important it is to share this elementary truth of self-sacrifice with new converts. I have seen how those individuals who willingly submit and surrender all of themselves to the Lordship of Jesus become dynamic and Holy Spirit-empowered disciples who are not only mightily used by Him but are also wonderfully blessed by Him in all they do and in their personal relationships.

God never purposed for salvation to be something that we take from Him with no commitment on our part. If you study the covenants God made with man in the Old Testament, you will find this same principle exemplified in most of the covenantal agreements made. The Bible contains more than seven thousand promises from the Lord, and most are conditional to believers acting out their part in order to walk in the manifested fullness of them. The opposite of being passive is being active. To be active is "having the power of motion or force; lively, brisk; effective, busy, operating; not quiet or latent; industrious; diligent." Hebrews 11:6 (KJV) says, *"But without faith it is impossible to please Him: for he that cometh to God must believe that He is, and that He is a rewarder of them that diligently seek Him."* This exemplifies the active nature of partnership with God. When we put effort into working with God, He works with us. The reward comes when we not just seek but when we **diligently** seek. To be diligent means to "persevere," which indicates that it will not always be easy, it will not always be comfortable, and to receive the benefit of the relationship will take effort and sacrifice on our part. That is what will add value to your partnership.

One definition of a partner is "one who takes part in an activity with another; one who dances with another." This is such a beautiful description of what partnership is meant to be. Dancing involves two or more people, moving in harmony and unity together. Biblically speaking, there are many passages that reference praising God in the dance. There is to be innocence, beauty, and love in the dance. Let's use the waltz as an example. In this dance, there are two partners moving together in unison and in harmony, with one leading and the other following. The woman must relax into the embrace of the man, allowing herself to be led around the dance floor. The man must gently draw her in, and she must be flexible in his arms; otherwise, she cannot be gracefully, elegantly, and powerfully moved around the dance floor.

It takes interconnectedness and partnership to create motion.

For motion to be created, muscles must contract. When muscles contract, they shorten; the joints move, and motion is created. John understood this concept when he said in John 3:30: "*He must increase, but I must decrease.*" When a muscle contracts, it decreases in size. To *contract* means "to draw close together," which is what must happen to create a fluid, flowing dance. Two individuals, each with their own personalities, strengths, and weaknesses, become one for the purpose of creating a beautiful and graceful harmony. What will happen if one of the dancers stops moving during the dance? The dance itself will stop. What will happen if a man comes up to a woman standing on the side of a dance floor, extends his hand in an invitation to dance, and she takes his hand but then refuses to move with him onto the floor? Just like in the dance, partnership is about motion—about both partners continuously moving forward *together*. Opportunities for new steps, new bows, new beautiful swirls and twirls can be missed if we are standing still, refusing to move. So it is with partnership. Too many times we enter into a relationship—we take the hand of partnership—but then we miss Divine opportunities simply because we are resistant to moving.

This same thing happens with the Lord Jesus and the leading of the Holy Spirit. Jesus is the Good Shepherd. He says that the sheep know His voice. It is the job of the shepherd to lead the sheep into fields of green pasture. To lead the sheep, He must take the sheep out of one place, through a gate, and on a journey to get to the next place. To get from point A to point B requires travel, requires motion. When we refuse to cooperate with the leading of the Holy Spirit, we again miss Divine opportunities for Jesus to lead us to greener pastures and places of safety and provision.

The partnership concept is one that God created from the beginning of time and how He also meant our personal relationships to be. God's intent and desire was to always lead man in the dance of life through the drawing of His Holy Spirit. It is the Holy Spirit that draws us into partnership with Jesus and Jesus who provides the way for partnership with the Father.

Partnership with the Lord, with His church, and with His ministers should be a beautiful romance—a perfect love story. A story not only of love but also of passion, dedication, commitment, support, unselfishness, sacrifice, dignity, integrity, laughter, and joy. It is about building a life together, creating a synergistic effect that the two together are better and stronger than the one alone.

It is by God's grace that I am able to share these wonderful truths with you, and as you read and meditate on this, I hope you realize that by that same grace, you can right now rededicate and recommit your life to Him and start with a renewed vigor to reach out, to seek ways and means to bless your existing partnership, and to prayerfully find new partnerships the Lord wishes you to enter into.

Chapter 5

ONE MOMENT IN TIME

In the events recorded in John 6:6-13, the Lord Jesus was teaching us another fundamental principle of the ordinance of partnership. There were about five thousand men that the Lord wanted to feed. (Including women and children, that would equate to approximately fifteen to twenty thousand.) One little boy came forward to present and to share his portion with the Lord and all the others—five loaves and two fish. Can you imagine this little boy? Here he had very little, yet he was willing to offer up whatever he had to the Lord. The Bible records that unless we have the faith of a child, we cannot enter the Kingdom of God. Can you imagine the faith of this boy? The disciples responded from a typical, intellectually cynical, unrenewed mind-set: *"But what are they among so many?"* Andrew saw the crowd, and in some way, scoffed at the innocence of that little boy. But the mind (faith) of a child believed that the little he had could somehow help all these people. He didn't look at the size of his offering. It wasn't a matter of how big or small it was. He simply had the faith to turn over what he had to someone his spirit recognized had the ability to use what he had to help someone else. The boy recognized he didn't have the ability, but Jesus did. And so in faith, he brought what he had to the Lord so He could give it to the others. He brought his seed, his tiny little seed, and sowed it into good soil—into Jesus' ministry—and in turn, into the lives of thousands of people he hardly or never knew.

Without realizing it, this boy was activating Genesis 8:22 and the Divine principles of partnership in his life. But the Lord Jesus knew! He accepted that offering as a priest on behalf of the Lord God. He prayed over it, blessed it, and then fed all fifteen to twenty thousand people. Not only that, but also twelve baskets full of leftovers were collected! So again, not only was that little boy sowing into Jesus' ministry, but he was also sowing into the lives of thousands of others. This represents twice-sown seed and, as far as God is concerned, twice the prophet's reward. That little boy had to give his offering to Jesus so that Jesus could prophetically display to His Disciples and to all subsequent generations the anointing of increase that has been bestowed upon those called of God as Shepherds to feed the flock.

This demonstration, this prophetic declaration of miraculous multiplication, was made as a blueprint for all who are God's called and chosen ministries to follow in feeding and caring for God's people. It's the anointing of increase and it is always activated when our giving is laid at the feet of God the Father, primarily with the intention of honoring Him as the Great Provider. The ministry is God's chosen vessel through which He will always work to increase the resources of His children. As children of God, we need to line up our thinking with God's Word, which says, *"Give, and it will be given to you. A good measure, pressed down, shaken together and running over, will be poured into your lap"* (Luke 6:38 NIV). That is why all of God's people, both in the Old Testament and in the New Testament, are instructed to bring all their tithes, offerings, gifts, and talents into the ministry, and then for these to be received as an offering to the Lord (being gifts originally coming from Him), and then for them to go out, multiplied in greater number than when they came in.

King David had perfect understanding of the workings of the ministry and that all things are from the Lord, for the Lord. Look at his prayer after the nation had brought their gifts and offerings in great abundance for the building of the temple:

Therefore David blessed the LORD before all the assembly; and David said: 'Blessed are You, LORD God of Israel, our Father, forever and ever. Yours, O LORD, is the greatness, the power and the glory, the victory and the majesty; for all that is in heaven and in earth is Yours; yours is the kingdom, O LORD, and You are exalted as head over all. **Both riches and honour come from You, and You reign over all. In Your hand is power and might; in Your hand it is to make great and to give strength to all. But who am I, and who are my people, that we should be able to give as generously as this? Everything comes from you, and we have given you only what comes from your hand.'** (1 Chron. 29:10-12, 14 MKJV)

Proverbs 3:9-10 (GW) says,

Honor the LORD with your wealth and with the first and best part of all your income. **Then** *your barns will be full, and your vats will overflow with fresh wine.*

In 2 Corinthians 9:8-13 (AMPL), we read:

And God is able to make all grace (every favour and earthly blessing) come to you in abundance, so that you may always and under all circumstances and whatever the need, be self-sufficient—possessing enough to require no aid or support and furnished in abundance for every good work and charitable donation. As it is written, he (the benevolent person) scatters abroad. He gives to the poor; His deeds of justice and goodness and kindness and benevolence will go on and endure forever. And (God) Who provides seed for the sower and bread for eating will also provide and multiply your (resources for) sowing, and increase the fruits of your righteousness (which manifests itself in active goodness, kindness and charity). **Thus you will be enriched in all things and in every way, so that you can be generous, (and your generosity as it is) administered by us will bring forth thanksgiving to God. For the service the ministering of this fund renders** *does not only fully supply what is lacking to the saints (God's people), but it also overflows in many (cries of) thanksgiving to God.*

The ministry is the arm of the Lord. As we learn in Acts 4:32-24, the gathering of the saints—being representative of the church—is the Lord's chosen vessel through whom, by whom, and for whom the Lord will always move to activate His anointing of increase. The Message translation of Ephesians 1:23 summarizes this concept flawlessly: *"The church, you see, is not peripheral to the world; the world is peripheral to the church. The church is Christ's body, in which He speaks and acts, by which He fills everything with His presence."* We as God's children should learn to enlarge our view—taking the focus off the here and now and shifting it to objectivity and, subsequently, eternity. Hebrews 6:10 (MKJV) says, *"For God is not unrighteous to forget your work and labor of love which you have shown toward His name, in that you have ministered to the saints, and do minister."*

In Proverbs 11:24 (GNB), we read an apparent anomaly of "normal" thinking. It says, *"Some people spend their money freely and still grow richer. Others are cautious, and yet grow poorer. Be generous, and you will be prosperous. Help others, and you will be helped."* Worldly thinking trains the mind to save resources, to gather rather than to scatter; in this way, we will become richer, having more to spend on the "luxuries of life." Yet here we find the exact reciprocal: the more we spend and give freely (as partners working together to promote His Gospel), the more we will be entrusted with prosperity. Again, this is in direct opposition to our carnal way of thinking, because often, God starts this process with an act that requires faith: giving out of our lack, not out of our abundance.

This concept of giving calls for a complete shifting of the paradigm away from our own definitions and intellectual abilities to the awesome miracle-working power of God. That shifting is faith in action and is the catalyst for creating the momentum to shift our focus from our own limited abilities to the unlimited abilities of the Lord. In Matthew 19:26 (CEV), Jesus said: *"There are some things that people cannot do, **but God can do anything**."* Our partnership with the Lord will move us into a new realm to the point where His values, His purposes, and His abilities become an integral part of our everyday lives.

It is time for His body of believers to understand the true context of the Great Commission as we find it in Matthew 28. We have been given a commission—a mandate—and built within that commission, the Lord has made provision for every need. This again is defined in Genesis, chapters 1 and 2. The Lord God first created Adam, then He created Adam's partner, Eve. With this partnership accomplished, He commissioned them both to subdue—to take dominion—of the earth as His representatives! By the time Adam and Eve were created, the provision for every need they might have to fulfill their commission was also already created; and so when they came to their point of need (to fulfill their Divine commission), they found the provision already waiting for them. The key the Lord gave us to walk in the manifested fullness of His already provided provision is found in Proverbs 16:3 (AMPL): *"Roll your works upon the Lord—commit and trust them wholly to Him. He will cause your thoughts to become agreeable to His will, and so shall your plans be established and succeed."* Verse 20 carries on to say: *"He who deals wisely and heeds (God's) word shall find good."*

When we are fully committed to the Lord through partnership, fully committed to help spread the gospel of the Lord Jesus Christ in all its many facets, we will then begin to understand the heart of the Lord. What is His heart? We find this all-encompassing answer in 1 Thessalonians 5:9 (AMPL): *"For God has not appointed us to (incur His wrath)—He did not select us to condemn us—but (that we might) obtain (His) salvation through our Lord Jesus Christ, the Messiah."* That is the very essence of the Great Commission we find in Matthew 28, and that is the mandate we—individually and corporately—are to pursue and publish with all of our hearts. When we do that, we will find, as we have explained previously, that even our thoughts will be influenced and directed by the Holy Spirit to lead and guide us away from our own limitations and to start operating within the miraculous sphere of His limitless provision.

In Mark 9:23 (BBE), the Lord Jesus heals a boy who was mute, deaf, and demon-possessed. It was obvious that the child's parents were desperate. He addresses the father's unbelief and made a profound statement: *"All things are possible to him who has faith."* The father said, *"Lord I believe . . . !"* and immediately the Lord healed and delivered the child. Our faith (in God) is one of the greatest treasures we possess on this earth. The faith declaration of the father was the catalyst that released the Lord's supernatural abilities in a limited natural world.

This very fundamental principle is again confirmed by the Lord in the events as recorded in John, chapter 11, where Lazarus died and his family buried him in a cave. Several days later, Jesus arrived to find Lazarus' sisters in mourning. He had them take Him to the cave where Lazarus was buried and told them to open the cave. The sister Martha objected, saying the corpse "stinketh"—had already started decomposing. Intellect, reasoning, "common sense," and . . . most importantly, doubt spoke through her. Jesus immediately challenged the definition of her (and everybody else's) reality. He replied: *"Did I not say to you that if you had faith you would see the glory of God?"* (John 11:40 BBE). Then with a loud voice, Jesus commanded Lazarus to come out of the cave, and against every possible human understanding, a living Lazarus did exactly that. They all saw the glory of God!

Our faith can move us into the supernatural unlimited realm of God, because it is with the arm of faith that we can reach out and bring His Divine supernatural Kingdom power into manifestation in this world. Our faith (in God and His infallible Word) is the catalyst that can cause the supernatural to become natural. As His disciples, His partners, in John 14:12 (MSG) Jesus substantiated this absolute promise to us: ***"The person who trusts Me will not only do what I'm doing but even greater things, because I, on My way to the Father, am giving you the same work to do that I've been doing.*** *You can count on it."* Can you see the instruction from Jesus to be co-workers with Him and the subsequent assurance that He will empower us with Divine abilities to fulfill that commission?

In Matthew, chapter 13, we find the reciprocal where great crowds were following Jesus, listening to His teachings, yet sadly in verse 58 it is recorded: *"And He did not do many mighty works there because of their unbelief."* It reminds me of the church today. The church—the body of believers—fills buildings on Sundays and listens to His Word, yet is operating by the same limited abilities, as was the boy's father prior to believing.

Let His words *"if you would believe you would see the glory of God"* echo in your soul, and act upon it with faith! You do not need a mountain of faith and a small God—you only need mustard seed-size faith and a BIG God. As a young born-again believer, I made a quality decision in my life that I want to walk in the fullness of that promise. I want to see the glory of God. I did—and I still do! Why don't you do the same and be completely transformed as you start operating by His power, His ability, His provision, His protection, and His unconditional love for you? Step out, become His partner according to His definitions, and see the glory of God!

Chapter 6

PREDESTINED OPPORTUNITIES

It is a medically admitted and proven fact that we are using on average only a small fraction of our mental faculties at any given point in time. The church today is operating under the same limitations because of disagreements, infighting, personal ambitions and agendas, lack of faith, and the absence of that harmonious symphony that will cause the Lord to move on our behalf.

As we have learned earlier, the very concept of partnership is of Divine origin. Unfortunately, because of its exponential potential to increase resources, partnership has been used and abused by the enemy (within the ranks of the body of Christ) to the extent that people no longer want to partner with "ministries" because their contributions were used and abused to build great personal kingdoms, instead of them being used for the purposes they were given. However, as much as we are aware of these unfortunate cases, it should by no means defer our willingness to continue to partner and cooperate with the Lord and use our provision and talents for the purposes they were given to us in the first place. Always remember, when we partner with a Holy Spirit-inspired and Holy

Spirit-filled ministry, we are, first and foremost, partnering with the Lord Himself. If those ministries then act irresponsibly with the provision the Lord has given them to fulfill His Great Commission, then He, the Lord, will deal with those untrustworthy servants in His time and in His way.

And let me hasten to say, as we've seen earlier, our provision should not always be interpreted in monetary terms. We have each been given talents and skills, and when we start availing these in partnership with others, momentum is created. **It takes interconnectedness and partnership to create motion!** This momentum is of great concern to the enemy because it will always have a "snowball" effect, which is exactly what the enemy is forever trying to prevent. As individual believers and as the corporate body of Christ, we have been given access to unlimited provision by the Lord to enable us to fulfill our mandate, but it is only when there is complete understanding of the power in unity that we will have the courage to step out and become involved in all the many facets of our commission. Why do you think we have the most perfect example of partnership ever—the Father, the Son, and the Holy Spirit, each working in perfect partnership and harmony with one another, being one, yet being three, yet being one. This perfect synergy should forever be our model!

Going back to the events recorded in John 6:6-13, I also want to draw your attention to something else the Lord established with this miracle of multiplication. He was able to multiply five loaves of bread and two fish—just enough to feed a few people—into enough to feed more than five thousand people. And not only that, but also twelve baskets were filled with the remains—enough for yet again a large number of people. I'm sure if anyone had the courage to ask the Lord Jesus to multiply the contents of the twelve baskets again, He would have done so—with much greater increase. The Lord Jesus was displaying the heart of the Father and His desire for us to start operating within His sphere of the supernatural when we become concerned for our neighbors.

This miracle of multiplication and increase happened *within* the ministry—not outside of it. It happened when His followers were harmoniously united with a common purpose. Also, the Lord Jesus could just as well have asked any of His twelve Disciples to pray, yet He chose to do it Himself, thus signifying His very personal involvement in the provision and multiplication of the resources for His people. As a matter of fact, in John 14:13-15, the Lord Jesus made us a profound promise:

> *Believe Me that I am in the Father and the Father in Me, or else believe Me for the very works themselves. Truly, truly, I say to you, He who believes on Me, the works that I do he shall do also, and greater works than these he shall do, because I go to My Father. And whatever you may ask in My name, that I will do, so that the Father may be glorified in the Son. If you ask anything in My name, I will do it. If you love Me, keep My commandments.*

This promise was clearly made in the context of His disciples having a need for anything for the purposes of spreading the good news of the Gospel. Jesus' intentions here are clearly depicted: He will personally see to it that every need is met.

We need to actively and aggressively pursue and expect His anointing of increase in every situation because we have His covenant promise for that. Becoming fatalistic in our levels of expectancy is not Christlike; on the contrary, it is exactly that attitude the enemy is propagating in order to promote his own devious agenda on the earth. The Lord's anointing of increase operating in and through our lives is a paramount requirement for us to partake in the joint venture of walking in the fulfillment of 1 Peter 2:9, as the ones called to bring into manifestation the goodness of God in this world, as well as the mandate to be co-workers with Him. Galatians 6:10 (NCV) says, *"When we have the opportunity to help anyone, we should do it. But we should give special attention to those who are in the family of believers."*

Partnership with a Holy Spirit-inspired ministry contains all the potential for an exponentially profitable relationship for all parties involved. It is vitally important that we be hooked up in unity through partnership with anointed praying people, because—as we are about to see—our individual anointings and our combined prayers of faith flowing in harmony in one direction with the rest of His body are far more powerful than any one of us alone could ever be: *"Again I tell you, **if two of you on earth agree (harmonize together, together make a symphony) about—anything and everything—whatever they shall*** *ask, it will come to pass and be done for them by My Father in heaven"* (Matt. 18:19 AMPL).

I am a great lover of classical music and can listen for hours and hours to the beautiful perfect harmonious sounds produced by the large variety of different musical instruments when the musicians all play together in harmony and purpose to produce a perfect symphony. The Lord is saying to us that our combined harmony of prayers and actions, working together in symphony toward a common purpose—His purposes—are so pleasing to His ears that *He* will do whatever we ask regarding the achievement of our (His) purposes! Why? Because when we, as His partners, also partner with one another, then we become the fulfillment of the Lord Jesus' prayer that we might be one as He and the Father are one. Our perfect symphony amongst ourselves is a perfect continuation of the Triune God—Father, Son, and Holy Spirit.

Remember, even though Paul and others were the instruments, it was the Holy Spirit who wrote the Bible, and it was the Holy Spirit who penned the will and intentions of God. He said in Philippians 1:3-5 (AMPL): *"I thank my God in all my remembrance of you. In every prayer of mine, I always make my entreaty and petition for you all with joy. I thank my God for your fellowship—your sympathetic co-operation and contributions and partnership—in advancing the good news (the Gospel)* from the first day (you heard it) until now."* Because of this, we can know that it is the Holy Spirit Himself who is always praying in perfect harmony, creating a perfect symphony, a perfect synergy between the will of God and our personal prayers; it is the Holy Spirit *"making entreaty and petitioning on our behalf"* because we are active partners with some ministry that is advancing the Gospel of the Lord Jesus Christ. Hallelujah!

Romans 8:27-28 (AMPL) confirms this:

> *And He who searches the heart of men knows what is in the mind of the (Holy) Spirit—what His intent is—because the Spirit intercedes and pleads (before God) on behalf of the saints according to and in harmony with God's will. We are assured and know that [God being a partner in their labor], all things work together and are (fitting into*

a plan) for good to those who love God and are called according to (His) design and purposes.

In 1 Kings 17:8-16, we read of the account where the Lord told Elijah to go and stay with the widow of Zarephath, whom the Lord appointed to take care of His prophet. Initially she, because of the desperateness of her own needs, was not willing to part with what she had left for her and her son. Yet when she became obedient to the Lord in partnering with His prophet, she reaped an incredible miracle, not only for the personal provision of their daily needs in the midst of a severe famine, but also in later receiving her son back from the dead! In Ephesians 2:10, the Amplified Bible says, *"For we are God's own handiwork (His workmanship), recreated in Christ Jesus,* ***(born anew) that we may do those good works which God predestined (planned beforehand) for us, (taking paths which He prepared ahead of time) that we should walk in them****—living the good life which He pre-arranged and made ready for us to live."* This scripture is very important to understand in the context of His Divine will in regard to partnership.

The Lord has predestined and preplanned those good works He wants us to do as we walk the different cycles of life. When we then reach that point of predestined opportunity (through partnership), we may *KNOW* that it has been placed there by the Lord with the intention and Divine potential to become the catalyst in a cycle of blessings in our own lives and which will be activated by our obedience to that Divine opportunity.

In 1 Kings, chapter 18, we continue to read how Elijah, by the Word of the Lord, left this widow and went on to humiliate and then destroy all the prophets of Baal in Israel. You see, God knew what He predestined and preplanned for Elijah to do, and He also knew the circumstances of the widow. He knew that unless she partnered with His Prophet, both she and her son would die from starvation. But not only that, He knew that her son was going to die from sickness later on. By His foreknowledge, God knew all of these things, and because He was the One who initiated partnership, He provided her with the opportunity through which He could meet her needs.

Through her obedience and subsequent partnership with Elijah, the prophet of God, she was actually partnering with the Lord Himself and, as such, played a pivotal role in the destruction of the prophets of Baal and in the process brought about the will and purposes of God. It was a perfect example of a limited human being used of God in a mighty way through a seemingly insignificant, simple action of partnership. The cycle started with the poor widow giving out of her lack; in other words, she gave in faith. It was the same thing with the little boy: he gave all he had to feed himself, trusting and believing in Jesus. **Partnership should always cost you**. Partnership requires that you step out in faith. It is when you give of yourself, as Jesus Christ did; when you are willing to risk, as Rahab did; when you give out of your little, as the poor widow at the temple did, that the principles and laws governing partnership are activated.

The widow of Zarephath responded to her day of visitation and reaped an incredible reward for it. In John 15:16 (AMPL), the Lord Jesus substantiated this principle when He said: "*You have not chosen Me, but I have chosen you—I have appointed you, I planted you—that you might go and bear fruit and keep on bearing; that your fruit may be lasting (that it may remain, abide); so that whatever you ask the Father in My name (as presenting all that I am) He may give it to you.*"

Did you notice the nugget? We are (Divinely) planted at a specific place at a specific moment in time in order to bear fruit for and in a specific season. This represents the perfect will of the Lord for our lives. "*Never walk away from someone who deserves help; your hand is God's hand for that person*" (Prov. 3:27 MSG). Psalm 37:23 (AMPL) confirms this principle again: "*The steps of a (good) man are directed and established of the Lord, when He delights in His way (and He busies Himself with his every step).*"

Remember in 2 Corinthians 6:1 (AMPL), we learned that we are appointed as "*God's fellow workers laboring together with Him,*" and so when we bear fruit, or in other words, when we respond in obedience to that God-given opportunity, knowing that our response was God-initiated and therefore within His perfect will and for His glory, then we ourselves may ask for anything in the Name of the Lord Jesus; and whatsoever we might ask, it shall be given to us. "*Ask in My name, according to My will, and He'll most certainly give it to you. Your joy will be a river overflowing its banks!*" (John 16:24 MSG). The Amplified Bible says, "*so that your joy (gladness, delight) may be full and complete.*" The widow of Zarephath was "planted" by the Lord at a specific place and at a specific time in eternity so that she might "*do those good works which God predestined (planned beforehand)*" for her.

Her obedience in responding to the opportunity of the moment was the catalyst that caused great abundance to be returned to her and her family.

We need to understand that it is not just about the "now." Our simple acts of obedience (or disobedience) have consequences that can affect generations to come. Had either that little boy or the widow refused the Lord's opportunity when their day of visitation came, their opportunity for blessing would have been lost. This simple truth is paramount in understanding partnership and our relationship with the Lord Jesus Christ. It is God's desire, His intent from the beginning of time, to partner with man to bring His goodness into this world. Jesus, when He sees a need, often will come to us, asking us to provide. When He comes and asks of us, what is our response? In Luke 19:41-44 (MKJV), Jesus weeps over Jerusalem, saying:

> *If you had known, even you, especially in this your day, the things that make for your peace! But now they are hidden from your eyes. For days will come upon you when your enemies will build an embankment around you, surround you and close you in on every side, and level you, and your children within you, to the ground; and they will not leave in you one stone upon another, because you did not know the time of your visitation.*

This was a very serious charge by the Lord Jesus. And it saddened Him because He knew the blessing He had in store for those who would respond in the day of His visitation, and so conversely, He knew the blessing that would be lost. Jesus said: "*A house divided against itself cannot stand.*" It is the law of reciprocals. In Matthew 12:30 (MKJV), Jesus says, "*He who is not with Me is against Me, and he who does not gather with Me scatters abroad.*"

Within the context of partnership and the blessings it affords, again it is important that we rightly divide the truth and, therefore, not miss our day of visitation. Often, we focus on the blessings without accepting the cost. We want the benefits that partnership provides, but we want them for free. Jesus Christ came and paid the price for our salvation, so yes, our salvation is "free," yet it is not. True salvation is not only believing in the Lord Jesus Christ but a complete walking away from the earthly kingdom's way of thinking and acting and walking into God's Kingdom values. This requires sacrifice on our part; in other words, to truly receive the fullness of the gift of Jesus Christ, we must give ourselves to Him _first_. This is true partnership in action, and it also applies to our human partnerships we establish. If we are truly Kingdom-minded and love the Lord with all that we are and all that we have been given and entrusted with, then we will be willing to step out in faith and give, without having received first, knowing that He will bless the work of our hands if our hearts are right before Him.

There are unfortunately many "ministries" within the body of Christ that will use fear, coercion, intimidation, manipulation, and lust for material gain to get you to partner with them and financially bless their "ministry." It is important that we rightly discern the Word of Truth, not being swayed by this doctrine or that or by the charismatic nature of any one individual or ministry. We need to be giving unto the Lord with the right heart motivation; otherwise, our giving is corrupt and will not produce the abundant fruit the Lord intends. We should never, ever give out of fear, coercion, or intimidation. This is the "mafia" approach. "Buying" God's protection or His favors or His blessing is not what giving or what partnership is about. Having said that, it is also important to maintain a balanced approach and to understand that God has set forth certain Kingdom rules. Our actions, or our inactions, are catalysts either way and do result in consequences God has set forth in His Word.

Let's go back and look at Luke 19 again. Here are the facts: The Lord Jesus Christ visited Jerusalem with the intent to visit them with a blessing (peace). But because they did not know the time of their visitation—in other words, they did not recognize an opportunity to partner with the Lord Jesus and, so, did not act—their inaction allowed opportunity for the enemy to come in and build an embankment around them, surrounding and closing them in on every side, leveling them and their children with them to the ground. Again, the Lord says, *"He who is not with Me is against Me."* We must understand that even though we may not be making a conscious decision to align ourselves up with the devil, by default that is what happens when we don't act in the day of our visitation. Think back to the definition of partnership we listed earlier: **Partnership is also companionship, friendship, and camaraderie, with the intent of surrounding one another for mutual benefit of aiding and protecting one another.**

Another benefit of partnership with the Lord is protection from our enemies. There are a lot of enemies out in the world that are actively working against us to keep us from receiving the blessings of God. Psalm 5:12 (NKJV) says, *"For You, O Lord, will bless the righteous; with favor You will surround him as with a shield."* A shield provides shelter and protection, which is exactly what partnering with a Godly ministry does. Through partnership, you become a shield to one another, mutually aiding and helping each other. But look what happens with the reciprocal of this, as outlined above. Do you see how, when we do not partner with God and Godly ministries and when we miss opportunities (which again means missing the day of our visitation), that now, instead of being surrounded by God, we are surrounded by the enemy, whose only desire it is to "steal, kill and destroy"? And not only us, *"but our children and our children's children."*

Just as obedience in responding to the opportunity of the moment can be a catalyst for great abundance, so will not responding be a catalyst for great lack of provision. Again, I want to make it clear that this statement is not made in any way to cause fear in you. Fear is NOT from God! But we do need to understand and rightly divide what God is saying to us and understand the ways of His Kingdom. Galatians 6:8 (MKJV) also very effectively defines this same principle and partnership with the work of the Lord and His Divinely appointed ministries when Paul says, *"Do not be deceived, God is not mocked; for whatever a man sows, that he will also reap. For he who sows to his flesh will of the flesh reap corruption, but he who sows to the Spirit will of the Spirit reap everlasting life."*

What does it mean to sow to the flesh? When we sow with the wrong motivation and for the wrong reasons, those are the things we will reap. Not sowing into the kingdom of God and spending all of our income on our own fleshly lusts and desires will also be sowing to the flesh, as the Scripture says. According to *Strong's Dictionary,* the Greek word for corruption in Galatians 6:8 is *phthora*, meaning, "decay, ruin, destroy, perish." So when we do sow with fleshly desires and intentions, we reap nothing of benefit in our lives and, in fact, reap quite the opposite. Romans 8:6, 8 says, "*For to be carnally minded [in other words fleshly minded] is death, but to be spiritually minded is life and peace. Because the carnal mind is enmity against God . . . those who are in the flesh cannot please God.*" However, if we sow to the Spirit, which means sowing for the right reasons and with the right heart motivation, sowing into good soil that will produce good results (those ministries that are already bearing good fruit for the Kingdom of God), we will reap a harvest of life and peace. Remember that sowing is all about partnership. You can have the best seed in the world, yet if you sow it in the wrong soil, your seed might still produce . . . but it will not produce to the measure or with the results that God intends—which is "good measure, pressed down, shaken together and running over."

People often ask, "I've sown and sown . . . where's my harvest?" In other words, they never see the result of their sowing. Often the answer of harvest lies in why and how we are sowing and what kind of soil we are partnering with. Remember: God has a certain "soil" that each "seed" needs to be sown into in order to produce "exceeding abundantly." What happens in nature if you plant a seed in the wrong type of soil? What if the soil is too acidic? Or doesn't have the right nutrients? Or is too dry or too wet? You see, the seed that we sow is only part of the equation. The seed itself can be corrupted, which obviously will affect the harvest. But the soil we plant into will also determine the size and quality of the harvest. Both the seed and the soil need to partner together in a perfect synergy in order to produce the optimum harvest. Too many times people in the body of Christ are sowing into ministries, programs, and events God never intended for them to sow into, because they were motivated by tradition, coercion, lust, or the charismatic personality of the leaders. Hosea 4:6 says, "*My people are destroyed for lack of knowledge.*" When you sow out of religion or tradition or coercion, you end up sowing into soil that may indeed be good soil **but not the soil intended and predestined and predetermined to receive your seed.** As a yardstick, it is good to always remember the Lord's guidance when He said: "*A tree is known by its fruit.*" That simply means the tree is not known by its shiny leaves. It is known by its fruit!

Remember: The Lord has predestined and preplanned those good works He wants us to do. God is Lord of the Harvest, and therefore God has already determined in advance the harvest He intends for us to receive. Ephesians 2:10 (MKJV) says, *"For we are His workmanship, created in Christ Jesus for good works, **which God prepared beforehand that we should walk in them.**"*

It is essential therefore that we sow into the correct soil as directed by the Holy Spirit to achieve the results God prepared beforehand. And each seed is different. Let me give you an example. Every Sunday you give an offering. Each offering is in itself a seed, capable of producing a harvest. If you sow into the same church, the same ministry each time without asking God first which soil this particular seed should be sown in to, what will happen? What kind of harvest will you receive? It is time that the body of Christ stops being destroyed for lack of knowledge! *"For he who sows to his flesh will of the flesh reap corruption,"* and corruption means "decay, ruin, destroy, perish."

Our tithes and offerings are what we present to the Lord Jesus as our first fruits and as a symbol of worship and acknowledgement of Him being our Faithful Provider, and we should present such gifts from grateful hearts. First Corinthians 10:31 says, *"So whether you eat or drink or **whatever you do, do it all for the glory of God.**"* The very fact that we have been enabled to earn a salary or an income should serve as an acknowledgement of His provision and grace. The key to sowing into the right soil starts with understanding that our tithes and offerings belong to Jesus and, subsequently, are no longer ours. We are simply to be obedient stewards of what now belongs to Him, and therefore it would stand to good reason that He should have the final say as to where He wants us to sow. *"It is a gift from God to be able to eat and drink and experience the good that comes from every kind of hard work"* (Eccles. 3:13 GW)

It is also essential therefore that we have knowledge—God's knowledge—in order to flourish and produce the harvest God intended beforehand. Proverbs 29:18 (AMPL) says, *"Where there is no vision [no redemptive revelations of God], the people perish."* Jeremiah 33:3 (AMPL) says, *"Call to Me and I will answer you and show you great and mighty things, fenced in and hidden, which you do not know—do not distinguish and recognize, have knowledge of and understand."* So what we need is for God to show us where that Divine connection is of soil meeting seed. We need to be calling to our Father and asking Him to show us and tell us His hidden things. Proverbs 25:2 (MKJV) says, "*The glory of God is to hide a thing; but the honor of kings is to search out a matter.*" God keeps things hidden and a mystery sometimes! Why does He do that? Look at Jeremiah 33:3. The "things" of God are "fenced in and hidden." Why would you fence something in? You fence it in to protect it. God keeps things hidden until the exact moment in time in order to keep our harvest from being stolen by the enemy, whom the Word of God describes as follows: "*Be sober and self-controlled. Be watchful. Your adversary the devil, walks around like a roaring lion, seeking whom he may devour*" (1 Pet. 5:8 WEB). The problem is that since we are not calling and looking to Him to reveal to us these hidden things, we are bypassing those hidden things out of lack of knowledge and vision. Much too often, we determine which field it is that we want to sow into, based on religion, doctrine, tradition, coercion, personal benefit, or love of material things; meanwhile bypassing the field that God actually already had prepared in advance to receive our seed.

Jeremiah 29:11 (AMPL) says, "*For I know the thoughts and plans that I have for you, says the Lord, thoughts and plans for welfare and peace, and not for evil, to give you hope in your final outcome.*" Look carefully at this promise, for this is just so wonderful of the Lord. God's intent for us is only good, and so He sets up circumstances in advance and then gets us into position to bless us. He wants to give us hope in our *final outcome.* Do you understand that you can only sow a seed once? Once that seed is sown, you cannot pull it out of the ground and sow it someplace else. Each seed we sow has a predetermined, final outcome that it is created from the beginning of time to produce. It is important to acknowledge, however, that just sowing the seed is not enough. In the natural, once a seed is sown, the farmer must tend the field—removing weeds and pests, keeping rodents and animals away, fertilizing, and watering. If we do not do these things with the seeds we plant, we are responsible for the limited harvest that may be produced. To repeat from earlier: "*For we are God's own handiwork (His workmanship), recreated in Christ Jesus, (born anew)* **that we may do those good works which God predestined (planned beforehand) for us, (taking paths which He prepared ahead of time) that we should walk in them**—*living the good life which He pre-arranged and made ready for us to live.*" God intends a good life for us, but we, as partners and co-laborers with Him, have our own part to play as to whether we walk in it or not.

The Lord has predestined and preplanned those good works He wants us to do as we walk the different cycles of life. When we reach that point of predestined opportunity (through partnership), we may *KNOW* that it has been placed there by the Lord with the intention and Divine potential to become the catalyst in a cycle of blessings in our own lives and which will be activated by our obedience to that Divinely orchestrated opportunity.

We also need to understand that, because the Lord has chosen the ministry as His chosen vessel through which He works, He will always want from us to work from and through this chosen body. Believe it or not, the ministry—the church—has the ability to change the world and everything and everyone in it, because the ministry is an extension of the Lord's hand in this world. When you partner up with a Holy Spirit-initiated and inspired ministry, whatever anointing of increase is upon that ministry becomes available to you. Not only that, but the reverse is also true. Whatever anointing (of increase) is on you becomes available to that ministry. When you understand that, you can see that when we all come together in partnership as the Holy Spirit directs, we'll all be fully supplied. In and of ourselves, we are incomplete. God knows what you need to complete your assignments, and He knows what each ministry needs to complete their assignments.

The anointing of increase will work both ways, and none of us will lack anything. See what the Lord has to say about this in 2 Corinthians 9:6-8 (MKJV): "*But I say this, He who sows sparingly shall also reap sparingly, and he who sows bountifully shall also reap bountifully. Each one, as he purposes in his heart, let him give; not of grief, or of necessity, for God loves a cheerful giver. **And God is able to make all grace abound toward you, that in everything, always having all self-sufficiency, you may abound to every good work.***" Spiritually, we'll have the full scope of the anointing of God, and materially, we'll enjoy the prophet's reward, joining in faith together to receive exceeding abundantly above what we can ask or think so that we may abound in every good work! "*He that receiveth a prophet in the name of a prophet shall receive a prophet's reward; and he that receiveth a righteous man in the name of a righteous man shall receive a righteous* *man's reward. And whosoever shall give to drink unto one of these little ones a cup of cold water only in the name of a disciple, verily I say unto you, he shall in no wise lose his reward"* (Matt. 10:41-42 KJV).

In Philippians 1:3-7 (KJV) the Apostle Paul wrote to the church in Philippi:

> *I thank my God upon every remembrance of you, always in every prayer of mine for you all making request with joy, for your fellowship (or partnership) in the gospel from the first day until now; Being confident of this very thing, that He which hath begun a good work in you will perform it until the day of Jesus Christ: Even as it is for me to think this of you all, because I have you in my heart; in as much both in my bonds, and in the defense and confirmation of the gospel, ye all are partakers of my grace.*

Notice in the last verse, Paul says, "*Ye all are partakers of my grace.*" In other words, Paul was saying, "As my partners, you share in the grace God has given me to fulfill my ministry." He was also telling his partners, "Hey, we're in this together and the grace (anointing) that God put on me to preach His Gospel is also counted for your credit because He has joined us together in partnership with Him (joint venture) for His Divine purposes and blessings." The word *grace* used here can also be translated as *favor*. Paul was saying that his partners would receive God's favor because they supported him in his God-given endeavors. Through partnership, the anointing, the grace, and the favor God has given us for ministry is also available to you, whatever your vocation.

You might say, "I don't need those anointings. I'm a teacher or an accountant or a technician, a clerk, a computer programmer, or . . ." That may be your profession, but let me remind you that, as Christians, we are **all** called to witness to people, pray for them, and minister to them; and the more of the anointing of God you have available to you, the more effective you'll be able to do it. The word *anointing* means "to be consecrated, to be ordained into office." So by default, it means to be Divinely enabled to perform a given task. God's anointing is by no means limited just for witnessing, praying, preaching, etc. It is also God's Divine enablement for you in your profession, whatever it might be, to excel and become the best. That is why the Apostle Paul could make the statement that those who support him are partakers of his grace, his favor. Obviously, that same favor will carry its own benefits. I have seen firsthand how God prospers His children, both as a corporate church and as individual members when they are active partners with Him in bringing His Word and His salvation to others—either directly or indirectly. Remember: "*You have not chosen Me, but **I have chosen you—I have appointed you, I planted you—that you might go and bear fruit and keep on bearing;** that your fruit may be lasting (that it may remain, abide); **so that whatever you ask the Father in My name (as presenting all that I am) He may give it to you**"* (John 15:16 AMPL).

God created each one of us to take dominion of and manifest His Kingdom and His good works here on earth. It is not just up to the "elect" few! We often leave the work of the "ministry" up to the ministers because "that's their job," yet we forget that when we become Disciples of Christ, the mandate becomes personal for each one of us to go out, make other disciples, and diffuse the fragrance of Christ everywhere we go. "*But thanks be to God, who in Christ always leads us in triumph—as trophies of Christ's victory—and **through us** speaks and makes evident the fragrance of the knowledge of God everywhere*" (2 Cor. 2:14 AMPL). We all need that Divine anointing of God to enable us to carry out this mandate, irrespective of our vocation.

Chapter 7

THE KING'S HEART

In 1 Samuel, chapter 30, we read the account of David and his men in hot pursuit of the Amalekites who burned their towns and took their women and children captive whilst they were away. David initially had six hundred men with him, but on their way, some two hundred men were too exhausted to continue with the pursuit. David left them to take care of their belongings. Those who went with David could then subsequently travel lighter and faster. After they caught up with and defeated the Amalekites and had their wives and children restored, they returned to the place where they left the two hundred. Some men in David's army were not happy to share the spoils they took from the Amalekites with those who stayed behind and, so, grumbled at the prospect of sharing. David, acting as the true king and prophet he was, responded in regal fashion when he said in verses 23 and 24: "*My brothers, you shall not do so with that which Jehovah has given us. For He has protected us, and has delivered into our hand the company that came against us. For who will listen to you in this matter? **But as his part is that goes down to the battle, so shall be his part that stays by the stuff. They shall divide alike**.*" The God's Word translation records his words as follows: "***Certainly, the share of*** *those who go into battle must be like the share of those who stay with the supplies. They will all share alike."*

Matthew Henry's Commentary on 1 Samuel 30:21-31 gives us further insight:

> Justice and charity must govern us in the use we make of whatever we have in this world. What God gives us he designs we should do good with, not serve our lusts with. The spoil we have is that which God has given us; we have it from him, and **therefore must use it under his direction as good stewards**. Let this check us when we are tempted to misapply that which God has entrusted us with of this world's goods. **God's mercy to us should make us merciful to one another**.

David understood this principle. He understood the heart of the Lord. It is no wonder the Lord said of him that he is a man according to His own heart. *"And when he had removed him, he raised up unto them David to be their king; to whom also he gave testimony, and said, I have found David the son of Jesse, a man after mine own heart, which shall fulfill all my will"* (Acts 13:22 KJV). The Bible teaches us that we, as believers in the Lord Jesus Christ, are considered by God in a very special, very unique way: *"He lets us rule as kings and serve God His Father as priests"* (Rev. 1:6 CEV).

That means we, as disciples of the Lord Jesus Christ, are considered kings in this world and are required to not only rule as such but also to act in accordance with that mindset. It takes a king in mind and heart to share his spoils with those who stay behind. It takes a true king in heart to understand that all men in an army serve together toward a common purpose. Only one who is truly such a king can then understand the importance of sharing the spoils of war with all his people. When we gain that measure of understanding, then and only then will we begin to act as kings and be true representatives of the Great King Jesus and will subsequently be awarded with more kingly gifts from on high: *"If you listen to what I tell you and live the way I show you and do what pleases me, following directions and obeying orders as my servant David did, I'll*

*stick with you no matter what. I'll build you a kingdom as solid as the
one I built for David. Israel will be yours"* (1 Kings 11:38 MSG).

This principle is the very essence of the Lord Jesus coming as Savior.
The way David dealt with the spoils in regard to his men was in royal
fashion. But now I want you to pay attention to his administration of
those gifts:

> *And David came to Ziklag, and sent some of the spoil to the
> elders of Judah, to his friends, saying, Behold, a present
> for you from the spoil of the enemies of Jehovah; to the
> ones in Bethel, and to the ones in Ramoth of the south,
> and to the ones in Jattir, and to the ones in Aroer, and to
> the ones in Siphmoth, and to the ones in Eshtemoa, and
> to the ones in Rachal, and to the ones in the cities of the
> Jerahmeelites, and to the ones in the cities of the Kenites,
> and to the ones in Hormah, and to the ones in Chorashan,
> and to the ones in Athach, and to the ones in Hebron, and
> to all the places where David had gone up and down, he
> and his men.* (1 Sam. 30:26-31 MKJV)

The first place mentioned where the spoils were sent was to Bethel. Bethel
means "the house of the Lord." The last place he sent some of the spoils
was Hebron, which was his home. So again we see David following not
only the Divine pattern of true kingship but also the Divine pattern of
partnership: first, with the Lord and then with his kinsmen. In his list of
priorities, his first thought was to provide for the House of the Lord; his
last thought was for his own house. David displays his absolute loyalty
to God and His Kingdom, acting as a true ambassador of that Kingdom
which he represents. He aimed not to enrich himself but to serve his God
first and then his fellow men and his country. God subsequently enriched
him, elevated him, and set him to rule as king over the same country he
had served.

Note also how he expresses the origin of the spoils. He called it *"the spoil
of the enemies of the Lord."* King David understood the principles of God's
covenant and partnership with His chosen people. The Lord considers the
enemies of His people to be His personal enemies, and David understood

it in exactly that way. He saw the enemies of Israel as not coming against Israel but, ultimately, as agents in satan's hand to destroy the people and purposes of God. In 2 Chronicles, chapter 20, we find the account where the Moabites, Ammonites, and others came as a very great army against the people of Judah. King Jehoshaphat, together with all the peoples, gathered before the Lord to pray and asked for His protection. Then the Spirit of the Lord came upon Jahaziel, and the Lord spoke through him, saying: "*Do not be afraid or discouraged because of this vast army, for **the battle is not yours, but God's**" (2 Chron. 20:15 NIV). Throughout the pages of the Bible, we find many, many examples of the Lord protecting and delivering His people, and He did so (and still does) because of their right relationship with Him. Partnership with the Lord through Jesus Christ assures us of a righteous relationship, protection from our enemies, provision in our time of need, and eternity with Him.

The same principles of partnership displayed by David were again confirmed by the Lord Himself in Numbers 31:25-31 (MKJV):

> *And Jehovah spoke to Moses saying, Count the prey that was taken of man and of animal, you and Eleazar the priest and the heads of the fathers of the congregation. **And divide the prey into two parts: between those skilled in the battle, who went out to war, and between all the congregation**. And levy a tax for Jehovah from the men of war who went out to battle: one soul of five hundred, of the persons and of the beeves, and of the asses, and of the flock. **Take from their half and give it to Eleazar the priest, a heave offering to Jehovah. And from the sons of Israel's half you shall take one portion of fifty, of the persons, of the beeves, of the asses, of the flocks, of all kinds of animals, and give them to the Levites who keep the charge of the tabernacle of Jehovah**. And Moses and Eleazar the priest did as Jehovah commanded Moses.*

Joshua also understood this when he said:

> *You are returning to your tents with your great treasures, and with very much cattle, with silver, and with gold, and with bronze, and with iron, and with very much clothing.*

Divide the spoil of your enemies with your brothers.
(Josh. 22:7-8 MKJV)

You might not be in the fivefold ministry, and so you think that ordinance doesn't apply to you. But it does! After all, you're a soldier, just like David's men were. You are a part of the army of Jesus Christ. You're on a mission to occupy this earth and enforce the devil's defeat, to empty hell, and to populate heaven until Jesus returns. Do not forget that when you gave your life to Jesus Christ, you also voluntarily signed up for military service. Signing up does not mean the commitment stops there. When you enlist in the military, part of the process is being trained and equipped for continuing service; and the expectation is that when the time comes, you will take up your position and fight. As stated previously, this again is part of what partnership with Godly ministries is about—getting you "ready for service." An army also cannot function without all logistical aspects covered and all positions being filled. What would happen if we left it up to just the officers of the military to fight a war? The war would be lost before it was ever begun! But that is what we do when we leave the work of Jesus' ministry up to the "official" ministers. Many ministries fail or do not walk in the fullness of God's intended purposes simply because the people of the army of God are not taking up their positions. ALL of us have a position to fill. Some are called to be "officers." Some are called to be "soldiers," out on the front lines every day. But those soldiers cannot work if they are not fed and clothed. Without a "support staff"—people operating as supply clerks, cooks, dishwashers, and administrative help—an army would not be able to function. Do not ever let the devil tell you that your contribution—no matter how small—will not make a difference. It could be the determining factor!

During World Wars I and II, many citizens from all the participating nations stayed behind and suffered severe shortages in their own lives to enable the soldiers on the front to take up their positions and fight. Those who stayed behind were also fulfilling a very crucial role in manufacturing and providing the frontline soldiers with ammunition, food parcels, planes, etc. It was not just the soldiers on the front lines that were actively waging a war—the entire nation was involved! You may not be on the front lines of the fivefold ministry, you may not hold the office of an Apostle, Prophet, Evangelist, Pastor, or Teacher; but if you are supporting a minister/ministry who is doing the work of God through active partnership, fighting alongside him/her through prayer, talent support, and through giving, you'll receive your due reward from the Lord for every person who accepts Jesus as Lord and Savior and for every believer who is strengthened, healed, or delivered as a result of that minister's endeavors. Remember King David, being a prophet, simply echoed the Lord's voice when he said, "*For as is the share of him who goes into the battle, so shall his share be who stays by the baggage. They shall share alike*" (1 Sam. 30:24 AMPL). The Lord then again confirmed this "law" in 1 Kings 11:38 with a promised blessing to the obedient.

I also want to remind you of the Lord's promise in Hebrews 6:10 (AMPL): "*For God is not unrighteous to forget or overlook your labor and the love which you have shown for His name's sake in ministering to the needs of the saints—His own consecrated people—as you still do.*" In 1 Corinthians 3:5-8 (GW), we have yet another promise: "*Who is Apollos? Who is Paul? They are servants who helped you come to faith. Each did what the Lord gave him to do. I planted, and Apollos watered, but God made it grow. So neither the one who plants nor the one who waters is important because only God makes it grow. The one who plants and the one who waters have the same goal, and each will receive a reward for his own work.*" In Ephesians 6:9, the Bible also tells us that the Lord is no respecter of persons. In other words, with the Lord, there is no distinction of "titles." We are all regarded in the same way, all loved with the same love and all treated in the same manner. We are all commissioned to spread the gospel of the Lord Jesus Christ, and therefore we will all be called to account for what we've done in this regard—or not done.

We also cannot withhold support or partnership from a "frontline soldier" just because he might not be from the same Christian denomination as ours. Such a person might have been appointed by God—whom we, as Christians, all worship and serve—and, in obedience, he will go and do what he has been called to do. The part of the body of Christ that is "staying behind" and is called upon to partner with such a person or ministry should assist through whatever means possible. That way, each one of God's children can become actively involved in the spreading of the good news of the Gospel of the Lord Jesus Christ. As believers and followers of Jesus Christ, we should never become so narrow-minded about our personal doctrinal beliefs that we lose track of the greater purposes of His Kingdom. As the body is made up of many parts, with each performing a different function, we should also understand that those with doctrinal differences to ours are also called to and often perform functions similar or different from ours.

Doctrinal differences are more often than not simply man-made rules based upon erroneous interpretation of the Scripture and might not necessarily be biblically correct. The deciding criteria, however, should always be measured by the biblical foundation of proclaiming Jesus Christ as Lord and Savior of our individual lives and also this world: only through His shed blood at Calvary do we receive forgiveness for our sins; through His resurrection and ascension back to the Father, He made a way for all who would believe; and through Him alone have we been granted access into the Father's presence. If a person or ministry would declare these elementary truths, then he or it would be deserving of prayerful consideration for partnership. First John 4:2-3 in The Message translation reads: *"Here's how you test for the genuine Spirit of God. Everyone who confesses openly his faith in Jesus Christ—the Son of God, who came as an actual flesh-and-blood person—comes from God and belongs to God. And everyone who refuses to confess faith in Jesus has nothing in common with God. This is the spirit of antichrist that you heard was coming."* And 1 John 4:15 (MKJV) says, *"Whoever shall confess that Jesus is the Son of God, God dwells in him and he in God."*

Just as we cannot place limitations on whom we partner with from a denominational standpoint, we also should not put self-imposed limitations on how many individuals or organizations we partner with at any given point in time. The deciding criteria should not be our understanding of how much we think is "right" or how much we think we can handle but should be the guidance of the Holy Spirit.

Partnership can be viewed much like a bicycle wheel. The wheel consists of an outer round rim and a central hub that are joined together by numerous spokes. The spokes themselves can be tightened or loosened for the purpose of keeping the wheel in alignment. In partnership, sometimes you are one of the spokes, and sometimes you are the hub. You may be called right now to just be a spoke, to just be connected centrally with one ministry. But God can also ask you at any point in time to become a hub, to extend yourself in partnership with numerous different ministries for His Divine purposes. As mentioned above, God is not a respecter of persons. He uses those individuals who have a heart for Him and for His Kingdom. Second Chronicles 16:9 (MKJV) says, *"For the eyes of Jehovah run to and fro in all the whole earth to show Himself strong on behalf of those whose heart is perfect toward Him."* If He calls you to partner with yet "one more" organization, He, firstly, is doing so for a reason and, secondly, will give you the know-how, grace, and means to see it through.

In this process of seeking the Lord's guidance in regard to our "connections," it is important therefore that we remain forever open and willing to His leading. We should remember the template—Jesus Himself. He partnered with all kinds of people from all walks of life and backgrounds. As mentioned previously, we must never underestimate the importance of anything the Lord asks us to do in regard to partnership. In the example of the bicycle wheel, all it takes is one spoke to be missing for the entire wheel to get a "speed wobble" or to become ineffective or unusable.

> *Dear friend, **you are being faithful to God** when you care for the traveling teachers who pass through, even though they are strangers to you. They have told the church here of your loving friendship. **Please continue providing for such teachers in a manner that pleases God.** For they are traveling for the Lord, and they accept nothing from people who are not believers. So we ourselves should support them so that we can be their partners as they teach the truth.* (3 John 1:5-8 NLT)

Chapter 8

DIVINE SEASONS AND CYCLES

At the same time we speak of extending yourself to partner with those whom God has called you to, we must also remember that everything in God's Kingdom works in seasons and cycles. Everything in God's creation and His governance of the universe speaks of cycles or, otherwise put, seasons.

A *cycle* can be defined as "a repeated sequence of events, time between repeated events, or a complete process" (*Encarta Dictionary*). The *Oxford Dictionary* says it is "the period of time taken to complete a single sequence of such events, a recurring series of successive operations or states, a series of events that are regularly repeated in the same order." This concept is very well defined in the Lord's Word, as we find it in Ecclesiastes 3:1-2: "*To everything there is a season, and a time for every purpose under the heavens: a time to be born, and a time to die; a time to plant, and a time to pull up what is planted.*" A process can only be defined as a completed cycle when the end meets the beginning. This is what life is all about on this earth. We live, we die, our children live, and they die, etc, etc. What we do or not do within the process of a cycle will have a direct effect on the outcome of that cycle and will have a determining influence on the following cycle. We, as parents, will face and have to overcome (mountains) in our lives—as a course of life. Every mountain we do not overcome will be left as an inheritance for our children. It is the spiritual and social responsibility of every parent to overcome (every mountain) placed within their life span, because either overcoming or not will have a direct consequence on the next cycle of events—those of our children. This is well explained in Proverbs 13:22 (NIV): "*A good man leaves an inheritance for his children's children.*" Psalm 37:22 (BBE) says, "*Those who have his blessing will have the earth for their heritage; but those who are cursed by him will be cut off.*"

Through many years in ministry, I have seen so many times how God's people get hurt because they do not understand the cyclic workings of the Lord. In this process, there are certain rules we should take note of:

1. More often than not, the entering into a new cycle is as a direct result of choices we make.
2. Once you are in a cycle you cannot get out until the cycle is completed.
3. When the cycle is completed, it's time to move on and into His next course of events for your life.

Partnership with the Lord and the extent to which we are yielded to the guidance of the Holy Spirit will always contain His infallible promise of helping, strengthening, and guiding us through the process of a cycle. In Hebrews 13:5 (AMPL), the Lord says,

> *Let your character or moral disposition be free from love of money [including greed, avarice, lust, and craving for earthly possessions] and be satisfied with your present [circumstances and with what you have]; for He [God] Himself has said, I will not in any way fail you nor give you up nor leave you without support. [I will] not, [I will] not, [I will] not in any degree leave you helpless nor forsake nor let [you] down (relax My hold on you)! [Assuredly not!]*

Some partnerships that God calls us to will be for a lifetime; others are only for a season. We must be sensitive to the Holy Spirit, to His leading, at all times. Sometimes the Holy Spirit begins to move in a different way or in a different direction and we either miss it, reject it, dismiss it, or rebel against it because of our emotional attachments, fleshly motives, desires, and understandings—or lack thereof. We must remember that every season has a beginning and an end. Ecclesiastes 3:1-2 (MKJV) puts this in perfect perspective: *"To every thing there is a season, and a time for every purpose under the heavens: a time to be born, and a time to die; a time to plant, and a time to pull up what is planted."*

Just as God can call us to enter into partnership, He can call us to end the affiliation because the purpose of why He brought and connected us with that person or ministry has been fulfilled. Too often, we stay "planted" with a person, church, or ministry longer than God has planned for us to. If we don't heed the leading of the Lord and therefore stay beyond God's season for us to stay, it can result in the relationship becoming unproductive and strained—on both sides. It also can result in us being out of position for God to connect us with the next course of events and His next orchestrated blessing in our lives.

It can be very difficult when a season comes to an end. Sometimes we can "see it coming," and so the transition is not so bad. Most of the time, however, it is not smooth sailing, and there can be numerous reasons for this. We get emotionally involved or financially or spiritually vested in the relationship, and so when God calls us out and away from it, we don't understand why or we may not see the reason for it. Often, in these cases, we "know" we are sensing the Lord, and yet, in our flesh, we don't want to sever the relationship because it seems to be "of God" or "advantageous" for us to remain. Conversely, our fear of man adds to the difficulty of walking away, because we are afraid the other person won't understand why we are severing the relationship, and we don't want any misunderstandings or hard feelings. In other words, we are more concerned about appearances, about what *they* will think about us than what God wants for us to do. As Christians, we need to understand and be obedient to the Lord's directive of when to stay and when to leave. Psalm 37:23, in the Amplified Bible, says, *"The steps of a [good] man are directed and established by the Lord when He delights in his way [and He busies Himself with his every step]."* We, as God's children, must understand and believe that the Lord is very much involved and takes a keen interest in all of our doings here on earth. We should be much more aware of this undeniable fact, become much more yielded and much more willing to receive His direction for every decision we need to make. Remember, He created us with the intent for us to receive a blessing!

God also has a way of sometimes closing one door and completing a cycle before He opens up another door. As human beings, we often want the security of having the question "Okay, if You tell me I am to leave this [church], where am I to go next" answered *before* we make the change. We want to be in control, we want to feel safe, and the unknown and waiting just doesn't suit us very well. But often, this is the way God works. That is faith in action. A good example of this occurs in Genesis 12:1. God came to Abram one day and gave him the command to *"go out of your country, and from your kindred, and from your father's house into a land that I will show you."* Can you imagine how Abram felt? How disconcerting that must have been for him, especially considering how family-oriented their culture was? I can envision the conversation now:

ABRAM: Okay, God. Where do you want me to go?
GOD: Just pack up your stuff and go. I'll show you along the way.
ABRAM: Uh, God . . . are you sure about this? Can you at least tell me the town I'm going to?
GOD: Yes, I'm sure. And no, just go.
ABRAM: Okay, well, can you tell me how long I'll be traveling for?
GOD: Until you get to where I'll show you.

God wants us to love Him and trust Him to follow His direction, even if we don't know where the next "there" is. We must remember that learning, growing, changing, and getting rid of "old baggage" often comes during the journey—not at the end. Anybody that's ever moved can testify about this. When we start packing, we wonder how and why we ever accumulated all the stuff that we now need to pack and normally end up getting rid of a lot of junk that we just don't need anymore. What is of vital importance is that we deal with every circumstance, every event, and every lesson we encounter during a cycle and not carry it forward as additional undealt with and unnecessary baggage. We are to make the most of every cycle, of every season, because each one is designed to equip us for His next course of events for our lives. It's like climbing a mountain. With every level you reach, you can see further and with more clarity and new motivation to move until you reach the top where the view is completely unhindered. Life is about experiencing the many facets of a diamond. You have to see the whole before you can appreciate the whole. We need to understand the reality of objectivity before we can understand the reality of subjectivity. Too often, God's people are so governed by the reality of subjectivity that eventually that (subjective) reality becomes the governance of the moment.

God delights in taking us from here to there and showing us all kinds of new things we never thought possible. He needs that "downtime" in between to prepare us for what comes next. No matter how it happens, when God closes a cycle, we must be willing to accept it and not get emotional about it, rather appreciate and value it for what it was. By closing one cycle, God is about to usher us into a brand new cycle. We must not be like Lot's wife, who looked back over her shoulder, longing for what was and missing out on what is to be.

We need to better see and understand God's hand in the process of change. Jesus Himself gave us an example when He took one substance—water—and turned it into another: wine. He constantly took eyes and ears that people had that weren't working, restructured them, and instantaneously made new cells to create new eyes and ears, more useful to the individual. He took a loaf of bread and some fish, blessed them, broke them apart, and then multiplied them to feed many. Jesus had a way of taking something, breaking it down, breaking it *apart*, just so He could use the pieces to form new structures more useful for demonstrating and promoting His Kingdom at that moment in time.

A perfect example of this from science is what happens in chemistry. If two molecules of hydrogen combine with one molecule of oxygen, a chemical structure called H_2O—or water—is formed. Conversely, if H_2O is broken apart, the individual molecules of hydrogen and oxygen are now available to join with other molecules to form other compounds, such as CO (carbon monoxide) or CO_2 (carbon dioxide) or H_2O_2 (hydrogen peroxide). God even designed the human body to do exactly this on a daily basis—ingest components; break them down; and then either eliminate, store, or recombine the elements for the good of the body. We, being the body of Christ, are fashioned and designed in the same way. If we are willing to listen and be obedient to the Lord's direction, irrespective of whether we understand the direction He is taking us or not, and irrespective of the sacrifice and/or cost that it may take on our part, God can join and partner us, even if it means breaking us apart first with the exact right other "molecules"—individuals and ministries—to form structures useful for His Kingdom's purposes in that season and time.

Conversely to this, it is also important to say that the exact opposite can happen. Many times God calls us to stay in a partnership we have committed to but that we don't want to (for various reasons—some good, some not), and so we leave prematurely. When this happens, either the ministry and/or we miss out on a blessing God intends for either or both but has yet to manifest. This blessing can take the form of something we perceive as "good" or can come in the form of "iron sharpening iron."

There was a time in my own life when I wanted to leave the church the Lord had me serve Him in for many years. As time went along, I reached a point where I became extremely frustrated and dissatisfied, and I desperately wanted to leave. It just seemed that everything pointed toward an "intelligent" conclusion that the season had come to an end and it was time to move on. I went to the Lord in prayer to seek His will. This is part of our submission to His Lordship over our lives, and as we just read in Psalm 37:23, the Lord will guide us if we are prepared to surrender our will (which is mostly based upon our assessment of a situation and which can be very myopic) to His complete objective guidance. Well, much to my dismay, the Lord told me to stay put. I can tell you I wasn't happy with that directive. I just wanted to leave, and all "circumstances" pointed me in that direction. However, what did the Word tell me? *"Trust in Jehovah with all your heart, and lean not to your own understanding. In all your ways acknowledge Him, and He shall direct your paths"* (Prov. 3:5-6 MKJV). If we truly surrender to His Lordship over our lives, then we should know that He would also direct our paths—for our benefit.

So many times the enemy manipulates circumstances around us to create a false reality. As children of God, we need to trust our Father explicitly and have absolute faith and confidence in His integrity and love for us. In Jeremiah 29:11 (AMPL), the Lord says to us: *"For I know the thoughts and plans that I have for you, says the Lord, **thoughts and plans for welfare and peace**, and not for evil, to give you hope in your final outcome."* Jesus

Christ is the Alpha and the Omega, the beginning and the end. All of our coming and our entire going should be for Him, by Him, and with Him. The Word of God always stands above whatever (subjective) circumstances surround us, and the Word of God should always be the determining factor and the final authority in the choices and decisions we have to make as we walk our (predestined) course, our cycle, of being His partners, working together with Him on this earth. In Hebrews 10:36 (GW), the Bible teaches us: *"You need endurance so that after you have done what God wants you to do, you can receive what He has promised."*

We have an enemy out there—satan—who is consistently working against us and who will continuously strive to manipulate circumstances to frustrate and influence us to make wrong choices and wrong decisions. The Lord Jesus warned us that this enemy is the father of all lies, that there is absolutely no truth in him, and that his intention is to kill, steal, and destroy all that God wants for us—even our lives. We need to have absolute faith, trust, and confidence in our God to believe that His only thoughts toward us are to bless and prosper us in all of our ways. This faith, this confidence, and this trust can only come through our building a relationship with Him through learning more about His person, His will, and His purposes. When we then step out and become active partners with Him, we begin to walk in the manifestation of His promises; and so our trust, confidence, and reliance upon Him turns into a wonderful personal relationship, which again is the essence of our partnership with Him.

In obedience to the Lord, I stayed. I stopped mumbling and grumbling, and I gave my partnership with that church (the Lord) more support than I ever had. The Lord is faithful (even when we are not), and I can tell you today that that one act of obedience to the Lord's will was used by God to provide me with an incredible miraculous testimony later on, and many, many people's lives were touched and changed as a result. In our "infallible wisdom," we quite often peep through the keyhole and think we have the whole picture and then, in our own self-righteousness, want to dictate to God what He should do next. I appreciate the Lord's patience and sense of humor when I think how absolutely absurd we are in our own limited wisdom when we think we know it all and have it all. God is already in the room—we are outside peeping in. He has complete understanding, complete perspective, and we need to trust Him more than our own judgment and understanding. First Corinthians 13:12 (KJVA) says, "*For now we see through a glass, darkly; but then face to face: now I know in part; but then shall I know even as also I am known.*"

Chapter 9

UNCOMMON ACHIEVERS

We have now seen that the very principles that we today define as partnership have originated from Almighty God Himself. The Lord Jesus embedded that desire in His prayer when He said, *"that they all may be one, as You, Father, are in Me, and I in You, that they also may be one in Us, so that the world may believe that You have sent Me. And I have given them the glory which You have given Me, that they may be one, even as We are one"* (John 17:21-22 MKJV).

Remember we have defined partnership as an agreement between two or more persons to collaborate, to team up, to join and work together toward a common purpose in a joint venture, and to unify and combine all abilities and resources in order to accomplish that purpose. Partnership is also companionship, friendship, and camaraderie, with the intent of surrounding one another for mutual benefit of aiding and protecting one another.

We, as co-laborers with the Lord, should remove every obstacle and apply ourselves in every possible way to assist each other within the context of partnership and to work and contribute toward an all-out effort to promote the lifesaving Gospel of the Lord Jesus Christ across the world. The only limitations to that glorious gospel are our unwillingness to work together and support one another and ourselves. No matter where in the world we find ourselves or whatever our occupation might be, as Christians, our first allegiance is to God, the Supreme Creator of all the earth. Everything else comes secondary to that. His priorities should become our priorities. If we are obedient to that, we ourselves will receive every conceivable blessing for the meeting of every need we might ever have. We have the Lord's promise in this regard in 1 John 3:22 (BBE): "*And He gives us all our requests, because we keep His laws and do the things which are pleasing in His eyes.*"

In Matthew 18:19-20 (AMPL), the Lord Jesus made us another promise: "*Again I tell you, if two of you on earth agree (harmonize together, together make a symphony) about—anything and everything—whatever they shall ask, it will come to pass and be done for them by My Father in heaven. For wherever two or three are gathered (drawn together as My followers) in (into) My name, there I AM in the midst of them.*" I want to draw your attention to two key words in these verses. The first is the word *together*, and the second is the word *for*. The Greek word used from which *together* is derived is *sonago,* which means "to be drawn together, to be assembled together." We find this same word used when the first disciples of the Lord were "drawn and assembled together" in worship when the Holy Spirit first came upon them, and great miracles followed. They were united in purpose, united in vision, united in their intent toward a common goal, and united in partnership with God and each other. The second word, *for*, which we find in verse 20, seems to be the determining factor for the manifest presence of the Lord. *For* introduces the condition for the manifestation of the promise, and the condition is the harmonious togetherness of His believers, His followers, with one mind and with one purpose.

When we would make a harmonious symphony as one, then He, the Lord Himself, promised to be in our midst; and when He is in our midst, love for one another, a oneness with the Holy Spirit, and a oneness with the mind and purposes of God will always manifest—for our benefit! That oneness, that complete agreement that forms the essence of partnership, is a sure foundation from which to direct our own prayers to God, with the subsequent guarantee of answered prayers. Not only that, but when you join up in partnership with a Spirit-led and filled ministry, you are one with them, and so you become the manifest fulfillment of the Lord's prayer when He prayed that we may be one as He and the Father are one.

In the introduction chapter, we saw in Genesis 2:18 the creation of a helper, a partner, for Adam. We saw the use of the word *azar*, which means "to surround, protect, or aid." In chemistry, the atom is the basic structure of every substance known to man—including man! Atoms form molecules, and molecules substances. An atom is composed of several different types of particles: neutrons, which hold a neutral electrical charge; protons, which hold a positive electrical charge; and electrons, which hold a negative electrical charge. Structurally, the nucleus, or center, of the atom houses neutrons and protons, while the electrons circle the nucleus at a high rate of speed. A question people often ask is "What gives this structure its cohesiveness and holds all these particles together?" It is known that any particle with an electrical charge will exert force against any other particle that has an electrical charge. It is also known that "like" charges will repel each other and that opposite charges will attract each other. In fact, with opposite charges, the closer the particles are to each other, the stronger the "attraction"—the bond or cohesiveness—will be. In the case of an atom, the "inside" particles are positively charged, while the "outside" particles are negatively charged. It is this opposite charge—this positive versus negative—that attracts and holds the particles together, just like a magnet.

Remember: It takes interconnectedness and partnership to create motion!

What a wonderful description from science of an existing biblical concept! Just as the electrons surround the nucleus, so we are called in partnership to surround each other. In a previous chapter, we spoke of the importance of supporting and aiding frontline soldiers, even when they are from a different Christian denomination. Just like with the atom, God might often call you to support an individual or ministry that is seemingly opposite of you, because it is when we come together with our different parts—our individual gifts and talents—that we become a cohesive whole. It is from the differences amongst men that we can understand the wholeness of God, and it is within and through partnership and unity that we see the reflection of God and can withstand the attacks of the enemy.

Two are better than one; because they have a good reward for their labor. For if they fall, the one will lift up his fellow; but woe to him who is alone when he falls, for he does not have another to help him. Again, if two lie together, then they have warmth; but how can one be warm alone? And if one overthrows him, two shall withstand him; and a threefold cord is not quickly broken. (Eccles. 4:9-12 MKJV)

Partnership with one another is the catalyst that enables common people to attain uncommon results and will subsequently transform common people into uncommon achievers.

Partnership with a Spirit-led ministry is God's way to double the potential of increase exponentially for both parties, so it is essential that you seek God now and find out whom **He** wants you to become a partner with. I encourage you, therefore, as you actively seek and partner with those whom God has called you to, to be as bold and courageous as that little boy with the fish and bread and as the widow of Zarephath, and start blessing those partners with and from the talents the Lord has given you. Then if you keep your faith hooked up with them, God will see to it that you're blessed with more of everything that you ever dreamed possible. God Himself will see to it that you receive the prophet's reward!

I thank my God in all my remembrance of you. In every prayer of mine I always make my entreaty and petition for you all with joy. ***I thank my God for your fellowship—your sympathetic cooperation and contributions and partnership—****in advancing the good news (the Gospel) From the first day (you heard it) until now.* (Phil. 1:3-5 AMPL)

EPILOGUE

We've learned through the pages of this book that partnership with the Lord and with each other is of Divine origin, with Divine intent as the catalyst to produce multiplication. This concept represents the heart of the Lord. He created Adam and Eve to have fellowship with Him and to be His representatives on the earth. He created them to work, to rule, and to subdue the earth in partnership with Him. He created Eve to be a partner and a helpmate to and with Adam and, in the process, once again established the blueprint for His Divine intentions.

When they both sinned and died spiritually, they were separated from His presence. However, even in their expulsion, the Lord promised them that the Savior of all mankind would spring forth from them. This Savior is the Lord Jesus Christ, and at Calvary—the cross—He accomplished the will of the Father: to reinstate mankind back into fellowship and partnership with the Lord God.

His death at the cross was a perfect example of the dynamics found in perfect synergy when two will partner together toward a common goal. His goal was for mankind to be restored into that perfect relationship with God that was His original intent when He created mankind.

When Jesus hung on that cross, He represented all of mankind and their sins—from the beginning of time till the end of time. He knew every person that was ever born, ever walked on the face of the earth, ever will walk on the face of the earth and subsequently took upon Himself the sin of all of humanity—that includes you and me! It was a price that none of us could ever pay, and it was a sacrifice that came at a very high price. He had to set the blueprint, the pattern to follow for all who would come after Him.

We have learned that Jesus Christ—because He was God's elected and chosen representative—became the only way through which man may come into the presence of God. There is no other way to be saved and to inherit eternal life but through Him. His act on the cross was the epitome of love, because He loved us first.

The cross consists of both a vertical as well as a horizontal bar. The vertical bar is representative of our relationship with God, and the horizontal bar represents our relationship with each other. The horizontal bar cannot be in place without the vertical bar. This once again points to God's desire to make peace with mankind and to restore man's right relationship with Him first, so that flowing from that relationship, mankind can enjoy a pattern of this Divine affiliation with each other in partnership. The horizontal bar is also "separated"—divided in two by the vertical bar—and the two "sides" become one where they are joined together by the vertical bar, until the entire cross becomes a complete cohesion. That complete union is what the Lord God had in mind when His Son was crucified: He hung on that cross, and He was the central force that brought all the loose ends together as one. He is one with the Father; we become one with Him and so, subsequently, become one with the Father. That way His people—His church—can once again become His appointed partners and representatives on the earth.

Every person is given the invitation and opportunity to receive the wonderful gift of salvation through the Lord Jesus Christ. If you have not yet received Him as your Lord and personal Savior, I would like to encourage you to do so right now. It does not take a long period of training or cleansing or "getting your life right first" before you make that decision. The Lord Jesus will meet you wherever you are, irrespective of what you are, who you are, or what you've done. He died on that cross for you, He was raised back to life again, and He ascended to heaven to prepare a place for you, so that you may have eternal life with Him and His Father. He loves you unconditionally—just as you are—and His heart's desire is that you will open the door of your heart and invite Him in as Lord and as Savior. He will never force Himself upon you because He loves you and respects you. He created you with the handle to that door being on the inside, and only *you* can open it.

Should you desire to accept this gift, then let me help you.

Pray the following prayer of faith out loud right where you are:

Lord Jesus,
Your Word says all have sinned, and so
I come before you as a sinner lost in my sin.
I ask You to forgive me of all of my sins,
all of my wrongdoings, all of my shortcomings.
You have shed Your blood at Calvary
that I might receive complete forgiveness of all of my sins.
Your Word also says You are the only way to salvation,
the only Savior of this world.
I now invite and ask You to become my personal Savior,
and I open the door of my heart
that You might come in and be the Lord of my life.
By my own free will I ask this of You,
and in faith I now receive your gift of eternal life.
Lord Jesus, I surrender my will and my life to You.
I ask, Lord, that You will cleanse me from all unrighteousness
and that you will use me as Your representative,
Your partner, to spread the wonderful news of Your Gospel
to all the ends of the earth,
so that the Father can be glorified through the Son.
By faith I now believe and declare that I am saved.
I pray this prayer in the name of the Lord Jesus Christ.
Amen.

If you have just prayed this prayer, then I would like to share some good news with you. In response to your prayer, the Lord Jesus said: "*I assure you, I most solemnly tell you, he who believes in Me—who adheres to, trusts in, relies on and has faith in Me—has (now possesses) eternal life*" (John 6:47 AMPL); and also, "*I am the door. Anyone who enters in through Me, will be saved—will live; he will come in and he will go out (freely), and will find pasture*" (John 10:9 AMPL).

That means you now have HIS assurance that you are truly saved, that you are now in right standing with Him, that you are now a member of God's eternal family, and that you will inherit eternal life. Nobody—not even the devil—can argue against the absolute truth of the Word of God, so don't let him come and tell you it cannot be this simple. The absolute truth is that when you accept the Lord Jesus Christ as your personal Savior, then you are saved—period!

I would also like to encourage you to share this new decision you have made and the new life you have inherited with someone you know—or even don't know. In Romans 10:9-10, the Lord says,

> *Because **if you acknowledge and confess with your lips that Jesus is Lord and in your heart believe (adhere to, trust in and rely on the truth) that God raised Him from the dead, you will be saved.** For with the heart a person believes (adheres to, trusts in and relies on Christ) and so is justified (declared righteous, acceptable to God), and with the mouth he confesses—declares openly and speaks out freely his faith—and confirms (his) salvation.*

Lastly, we would like to hear from you and celebrate this most momentous day of your earthly life together with you, so please visit our website and use the "Contact Us" page to write to us.

Stay very excessively blessed in all of your coming and in all of your going. We pray the Lord's Divine favor goes before you and that He will make level paths for your feet. We pray the Lord will bless your work of faith in partnership with Him and His people and that He will use you mightily as His partner to proclaim this glorious message of salvation throughout the whole earth.

We pray the Lord will use your partnership with Him to also bless you in your earthly partnership/s.

Stay blessed!

Izak Bester

PARTNERSHIP INVITATION

Dear reader,

I am the Founder and President of Eagle Christian Ministries International, a ministry with a prophetic mandate. ECMI is conceived, birthed and called of God and is chosen, ordained and appointed by Him to be one of His voices in the wilderness, fulfilling the foundational position of prophet within the body of Christ. The prophet plays a pivotal role in the process of God's intervention in the affairs of mankind. Throughout the ages, God has uniquely used His prophets to steer the course of nations; to bring encouragement, correction, and direction to His people; to bring clarity, interpretation and understanding of His ways, His Word, and His nature; and to re-present Jesus Christ, the One True Prophet, to a world that is in need of knowing Him. The prophet not only has the ability to see in the future and bring what he sees into the present, but also has the ability to help individuals understand how to apply what he sees in their lives and circumstances. A true prophet of God speaks the Word of God without compromise because God is much more concerned about our character, dignity, and integrity as Christians than our comfort.

Currently, the United States (and the world) is at a precipitous moment in time. She, like the Israelites of old, has turned her back on God in many ways and the Lord, as with the Israelites, is setting His plumb line in place and calling her back to her roots in Himself. The Lord has shown me snapshots of an unprecedented move of the Holy Spirit coming upon the USA and parts of the northern hemisphere. He has commissioned me to raise up the fire-carriers He will use in this great move and to declare His Word to nations, governments, churches, and individuals in preparation of this great coming move.

God has called ECMI to be an itinerant ministry, just as prophets often were throughout the bible because of their unique calling, and therefore we are not geographically or denominationally limited. We are fulfilling our commission across all denominations locally and internationally through invitations to minister, through prophetic teachings, seminars and conventions, and through literary and audio teaching materials. We are also working at establishing new congregations wherever the Lord leads and assisting currently established churches overseas that are in need of financial and spiritual leadership and support. We are called, just as the Old Testament temple was, to be a storehouse, where people can come and receive provision and then take out to others what they have received.

In order to accomplish our calling, ECMI needs to partner with local established churches, ministries, businesses, and individuals to bring forth God's word specific to their members, city, and region and to have them partner with us, so that we may support each other in all aspects.

God does not do anything without telling His prophets first. Many people have been crying out for a move of God, yet they often forget that when God moves, He cleanses and purifies. We also forget that satan will always try and thwart the move of God, and times of difficulty, trial, and testing are a reality. The true prophet of God is not a luxury or add-on in this time, but a necessity for success, prosperity, and survival.

It is imperative that we continue to speak the declared word of the Lord and that we are enabled to prepare His people through training and timely words of wisdom, insight and guidance for what is coming.

As an itinerant ministry, we need God's appointed people to partner with us, to help us and support us in all aspects. Just as in the cases of Moses, Solomon, and Nehemiah, we need help in the form of gifts, talents, finances, expertise, prayers, and more to declare the awesome power of God's Word into a world that is becoming increasingly dark. Only His Word can lift the veil of darkness; only His word can change our realities so that we—His people—can see and be prepared to become useful instruments in His hands.

As we have seen throughout this book, partnership is of Godly origin and is a mandate from the Lord for all of His followers with the specific intent to increase the resources, abilities and rewards for the body of Christ as a whole and for every believer individually.

Partnership *is* God's way for success, prosperity, and survival.

We need each other!!

If the Lord has laid the desire on your heart to stand and partner with ECMI and myself, then please visit our website at: www. eaglechristianministriesint.com, go to "Partner sign up" page, and send us your information. You may also use the "Contact Us" page to tell us how you want to honor the Lord with the gifts and talents He gave you through your partnership with us. Please feel free to also spend time on all the other pages of our website . . . you'll be blessed!

Stay blessed!

Izak Bester

Printed in the USA
CPSIA information can be obtained
at www.ICGtesting.com
LVHW091016131223
766396LV00006B/169